Greek and Latin Roots

Teaching Vocabulary to Improve Reading Comprehension

Written by
Trisha Callella

Editor: Sheri Rous

Cover Illustrator: Barbara Peterson

Designer/Production: Barbara Peterson/Carmela Murray

Cover Designer: Barbara Peterson

Art Director: Tom Cochrane

Project Director: Carolea Williams

Reprinted 2009

© 2004 Creative Teaching Press, Inc., Huntington Beach, CA 92649

Reproduction of activities in any manner for use in the classroom and not for commercial sale is permissible.
Reproduction of these materials for an entire school or for a school system is strictly prohibited.

Table of Contents

Introduction 3

Getting Started 4

Planning and Scheduling
Teaching a Lesson

Greek and Latin Roots

ped (foot) 7

man, manu (hand) 11

Review Test 15

spec (see, look) 16

dict (speak) 20

Review Test 24

ject (throw) 25

sect (cut; separate) 29

Review Test 33

port (carry) 34

miss, mit (send) 38

Review Test 42

graph (writing) 43

scrib, script (write) 47

Review Test 51

cred (believe) 52

jur, jus, jud (law; justice) 56

Review Test 60

ben, bene, bon (good, well) 61

mal, male (bad; abnormal; worse) 65

Review Test 69

bio (life) 70

vit, viv (live; life) 74

Review Test 78

flect, flex (bend) 79

frail, fract, frag (break; shatter) 83

Review Test 87

junct, join, jug (to join, meet, or link) . . 88

rupt (break) 92

Review Test 96

cede, ceed, cess (go; yield) 97

vers, vert (turn) 101

Review Test 105

tract (pull) 106

struct (build) 110

Review Test 114

therm (heat, temperature) 115

socio (companion, friend) 119

Review Test 123

phon, phono, phone (sound, voice) . . . 124

strain, strict, string (bind, tie, or
        draw tight) 128

Review Test 132

terr, terra, geo (land; earth) 133

naut, naus, nav (relating to the sea,
        ships, or travelers) 137

Review Test 141

Answer Key 142

Introduction

Many students are good "decoders"—they know how to read a word by sounding out its parts. But often their comprehension of the word's meaning isn't as strong. All of the research in the area of comprehension agrees that a strong vocabulary is the foundation for reading comprehension. In fact, vocabulary is the foundation of all areas of literacy—listening, speaking, reading, and writing.

Since increasing and developing a student's vocabulary will improve his or her overall reading comprehension, research recommends teaching students the parts of words. Beginning at grade three the national standards require that students use their knowledge of prefixes and suffixes to determine the meaning of words, and that they use their knowledge of root words to determine the meaning of unknown words within a passage. All words are made up of prefixes, roots, and/or suffixes. They are the meaningful chunks in every word a student reads. Too often, students skip words they don't know as they are reading. This breaks down their understanding of the text. For this reason, students need to learn how to break down the meaningful parts of unknown words so they won't skip them. This is especially important for multisyllabic words. By teaching your students how to "dissect" words using the lessons in *Greek and Latin Roots,* they will learn how to comprehend multisyllabic words, not just decode them.

The activities in this resource incorporate all levels of literacy to maximize the transfer of vocabulary into your students' speech, writing, and reading comprehension.

Each lesson has four activity pages to teach students new vocabulary and thereby improve their comprehension skills:

- A take-home **Word List** with parts of speech to study.
- A set of hands-on **Vocabulary Sort cards** to match up for independent practice.
- A set of **Read-Around Review game cards** for small-group review and transfer of what was learned. (The definitions are rewritten in this game, so students have to think and apply what they have learned about the meanings of words. This game combines listening, speaking, and reading.)
- A **Vocabulary Quiz** using test-prep and fill-in-the blank formats that require thinking, reading, and writing. The questions extend students' learning.

Getting Started

Planning and Scheduling

The most important thing to remember when learning anything is review. Ideally, your students will overlearn these roots, so that they become second nature to them. Your students will become increasingly more confident in their ability to understand larger words as they become more comfortable with "dissecting" words and defining the parts of words. The best part is that students will start using the vocabulary words you teach in their oral language and in their writing! The key is incorporating ongoing review activities and games into your everyday curriculum.

Adopt the motto "New, New, Review" in your classroom. This motto is so key to the success of building vocabulary that will transfer to all areas of literacy that this book is arranged in this exact format. For every Greek and Latin root, there is a review test. This serves as an easy way for you to remember that ongoing review opportunities are critical to the transfer of learning.

Teach one root each week, which will lead to a three-week teaching cycle. For example, you would teach a new root week 1, a new root week 2, and review the two roots during week 3. The review tests included in this book for each pair of roots will make this schedule easy to follow. Read the information on pages 5 and 6 for directions on how to implement each lesson. Use the following Suggested Weekly Plan to help you organize and plan your teaching of Greek and Latin roots and new vocabulary.

 Suggested Weekly Plan

Day 1: **Introduce vocabulary** in a pocket chart.
Pass out **Word Lists** for students to take home.
Play a **game** with the new words (see page 6).

Day 2: **Review vocabulary** in the pocket chart.
Play **Vocabulary Sort.**

Day 3: **Review vocabulary** in the pocket chart.
Play a **game** with the vocabulary words (see page 6).
Use the **Read-Around Review game cards** with small groups.

Day 4: **Review vocabulary** in the pocket chart.
Play a **game** with the vocabulary words (see page 6).
Use the **Read-Around Review game cards** with small groups.
Have **students make up questions** they think will be on the vocabulary quiz.

Day 5: **Review vocabulary** in the pocket chart.
Play a **game** with the vocabulary words (see page 6).
Have students take the **Vocabulary Quiz.**

Teaching a Lesson

Word List (Days 1–5)

Each lesson begins with a word list of ten vocabulary words that contain the Greek or Latin root that is the focus for the lesson. Each list includes the part of speech and the definition for each word. Send these lists home for students to practice reading with their family.

- Introduce, teach, and review each set of vocabulary words by typing each word in a large font size and printing it on a piece of construction paper (quarter sheet of 12" x 18" or 30.5 cm x 46 cm construction paper). Do the same for each definition. Display these enlarged word cards in a large pocket chart for hands-on manipulation and practice. At the end of each week, place the cards together on a ring, and neatly store them in a shoe organizer that has clear pockets. Students can play games with the cards independently or with partners. It will make a big difference in their learning!

- Display only the words in the pocket chart. Read each word, and have students repeat it so their pronunciation is correct. Clap the number of syllables while rereading the words again. Read one definition at a time so students can apply logic and deduction to figure out which word it defines.

- After students have had the opportunity to pronounce the words correctly several times, invite them to write the words on the board with the correct syllable breaks.

Vocabulary Sort (Day 2)

Following the list of root words and their definitions is a list of the same ten words and definitions mixed up and arranged on cut-apart slips of paper. This activity is intended to provide hands-on practice with the words.

- Copy a class set of Vocabulary Sort cards on construction paper or tagboard, cut apart the words and definitions, and place each set in a resealable plastic bag or small envelope. (You may want to laminate the cards for greater durability.) Have students independently match the words and definitions. Invite them to check their work by referring to their word list.

- Give each student a large envelope to store his or her Vocabulary Sort cards in after taking the quiz for that lesson. Have students add sets of cards to this collection all year long. At least once every two weeks, give students time to match up all of the root words and definitions they have learned. Although this will be challenging, the review will enhance students' vocabulary as they continue to use words they learned in previous lessons.

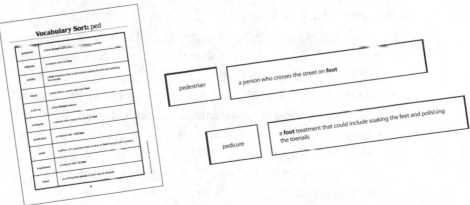

Read-Around Review (Days 3–4)

This set of cards includes definitions for all ten words that broaden the definition and apply more specifically to a practical context. Use these cards to play an interactive game with your students.

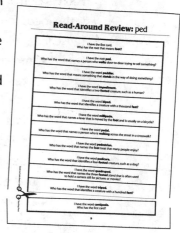

- Copy a set of cards on construction paper or tagboard for each small group of students. Cut apart the cards, and laminate them. Place each set of cards in an envelope, and write the title (e.g., *phono*) on it. Give each group a set of cards so that each student has several cards. Read aloud each student's cards, and then have students silently read their cards at least five times. Discuss each question and corresponding answer so students are familiar and comfortable with all the cards. Tell the group that the student who has the clue card that says *I have the first card* will begin the game by reading aloud his or her card. After the first card is read aloud, have the student with the answer to the clue read aloud his or her card. Tell students to continue until they get back to the first card.

Games (Days 1, 3, 4, 5)

- **Around the World:** Display the words in a pocket chart, and hold the definitions in your hand. Have students stand in 2–5 lines behind each other. Read a definition. The first student to say the matching word moves to the back of the line. Continue until each student has had several turns. This game is terrific for review weeks when you can use many different sets of root words. (Store cards on rings for easy flipping.)
- **VOCABO:** Give each student a blank piece of paper. Have students draw lines to make a 4 x 4 grid of boxes (three lines across and three lines down). Tell them to write the vocabulary words and roots in any boxes they want as you say the words. Say one word at a time. Have students repeat it. Spell it out for them to write down by syllables. Include words studied in previous lessons for ongoing review. (Students love having a "free space" on their board!) After students' boards are filled in, play as you would play BINGO.
- **Vocabulary Race:** Put all of the words and definitions in a pocket chart. Invite two students to go up to the pocket chart. Give each student half of the definitions or words. Set a timer, and say *GO!* Have the students race to match up all of their words and definitions. Invite the remaining students to sit at their desks and watch for errors.

Assessment (Day 5)

- **Vocabulary Quiz:** Use the 15-question quiz at the end of each lesson to assess students' learning. The quizzes include fill-in-the-bubble and fill-in-the-blank questions to help prepare students for standardized tests.
- **Review Test:** A 15-question review test follows every two lessons. Each test assesses students' knowledge using a fill-in-the-bubble format. Some review tests may contain questions that rely on students to use prior knowledge about prefixes or suffixes to answer. These questions are set apart with an asterisk (*). These questions can be used to assess students on their understanding of prefixes and suffixes, as extra credit, or as a supplement for more advanced students.

Word List: ped = foot

Vocabulary	Definitions
biped (n)	a creature with two **feet**
centipede (n)	a creature with 100 **feet**
impediment (n)	something that **stands** in one's way; an obstacle
millipede (n)	a creature with 1,000 **feet**
pedal (n)	a lever that is moved with one's **foot**
peddler (n)	a person who goes from door to door on **foot** trying to sell a product
pedestrian (n)	a person who walks across the street on **foot**
pedicure (n)	a **foot** treatment that could include soaking the feet and polishing the toenails
quadruped (n)	a four-**footed** creature
tripod (n)	a three-**footed** stand often used to balance a camera

Greek and Latin Roots © 2004 Creative Teaching Press

Vocabulary Sort: ped

pedestrian	a three-**footed** stand often used to balance a camera
millipede	a creature with two **feet**
peddler	a **foot** treatment that could include soaking the feet and polishing the toenails
tripod	a lever that is moved with one's **foot**
pedicure	a four-**footed** creature
centipede	a person who crosses the street on **foot**
quadruped	a creature with 1,000 **feet**
pedal	a person who goes from door to door on **foot** trying to sell a product
impediment	a creature with 100 **feet**
biped	something that **stands** in one's way; an obstacle

Greek and Latin Roots © 2004 Creative Teaching Press

Read-Around Review: ped

I have the first card.
Who has the root that means **foot?**

I have the root **ped.**
Who has the word that names a person who **walks** door-to-door trying to sell something?

I have the word **peddler.**
Who has the word that means something that **stands** in the way of doing something?

I have the word **impediment.**
Who has the word that identifies a two-**footed** creature, such as a human?

I have the word **biped.**
Who has the word that identifies a creature with a thousand **feet?**

I have the word **millipede.**
Who has the word that names a lever that is moved by the **foot** and is usually on a bicycle?

I have the word **pedal.**
Who has the word that names a person who is **walking** across the street in a crosswalk?

I have the word **pedestrian.**
Who has the word that names the **foot** treat that many people enjoy?

I have the word **pedicure.**
Who has the word that identifies a four-**footed** creature, such as a dog?

I have the word **quadruped.**
Who has the word that names the three-**footed** stand that is often used
to hold a camera still for pictures or movies?

I have the word **tripod.**
Who has the word that identifies a creature with a hundred **feet?**

I have the word **centipede.**
Who has the first card?

Greek and Latin Roots © 2004 Creative Teaching Press

Name _____ Date _____

Vocabulary Quiz: ped

Shade in the bubble for the correct word.

Ⓐ Ⓑ Ⓒ Ⓓ **1.** Cats and dogs are examples of these.
A) quadrupeds B) bipeds C) tripods D) peddlers

Ⓐ Ⓑ Ⓒ Ⓓ **2.** Janet took her daughter to get one of these so her toes would look pretty for the summer.
A) pedestrian B) pedicure C) millipede D) impediment

Ⓐ Ⓑ Ⓒ Ⓓ **3.** Let's put the camera on this so that it won't wiggle as much!
A) quadruped B) peddler C) pedestrian D) tripod

Ⓐ Ⓑ Ⓒ Ⓓ **4.** Most bicycles have two of these that make the wheels turn around.
A) pedals B) peddlers C) impediments D) pedestrians

Ⓐ Ⓑ Ⓒ Ⓓ **5.** Gerald looked through the peek hole in his front door and saw one of these holding a box of candy.
A) pedestrian B) millipede C) quadruped D) peddler

Ⓐ Ⓑ Ⓒ Ⓓ **6.** Did you see Chloe's pet? It must have a thousand legs! It's one of these.
A) centipede B) quadruped C) millipede D) biped

Ⓐ Ⓑ Ⓒ Ⓓ **7.** Logan, Zack, and Ryan are smart. They always look both ways and use crosswalks. What are they?
A) peddlers B) pedestrians C) centipedes D) quadrupeds

Ⓐ Ⓑ Ⓒ Ⓓ **8.** Tanya jumped when she saw one of these crawling across her living room! She's sure it had a hundred legs!
A) centipede B) millipede C) biped D) quadruped

Ⓐ Ⓑ Ⓒ Ⓓ **9.** Although Marissa walked with a limp, she didn't let this _____ get in her way.
A) impediment B) pedestrian C) peddler D) pedicure

Ⓐ Ⓑ Ⓒ Ⓓ **10.** Most of these living things walk upright rather than crawling.
A) bipeds B) quadrupeds C) millipedes D) peddlers

Write the correct word on the line so the sentence makes sense.

11. Tristan's speech _____ lessened every year, so people could hear his words more clearly when he gave his graduation speech.

12. The _____ were trying to earn money for their trip.

13. On the road, drivers must always watch out for _____.

14. Suzanne had to cut back on her monthly spending, so she could not go to the spa for a _____.

15. Rabbits would be classified as _____, not _____.

Greek and Latin Roots © 2004 Creative Teaching Press

Word List: man, manu = hand

Vocabulary	Definitions
emancipate (v)	to set free; to lend a **hand** in freeing someone; to release from someone's **hands**
manacles (n)	**handcuffs**
manager (n)	a person who has the upper **hand;** a person who is in charge of someone or something
mandate (n)	an order or command placed in one's **hands**
maneuver (v)	to **handily** or skillfully go around something
manicure (n)	a treatment for the **hands** and nails
manipulate (v)	to skillfully operate by **hand**
manual (n)	a **handbook;** a book of directions
manufacture (v)	to make by **hand** or by machine; to change raw material into a new product
manuscript (n)	a **handwritten** or typed piece of writing, such as a book

Greek and Latin Roots © 2004 Creative Teaching Press

Vocabulary Sort: man, manu

manipulate	a **handbook;** a book of directions
manicure	to make by **hand** or by machine; to change raw material into a new product
manacles	to set free; to lend a **hand** in freeing someone; to release from someone's **hands**
maneuver	an order or command placed in one's **hands**
manufacture	a person who has the upper **hand;** a person who is in charge of someone or something
manuscript	to skillfully operate by **hand**
manual	**handcuffs**
emancipate	to **handily** or skillfully go around something
manager	a **handwritten** or typed piece of writing, such as a book
mandate	a treatment for the **hands** and nails

Greek and Latin Roots © 2004 Creative Teaching Press

Read-Around Review: man, manu

I have the first card.
Who has the roots that mean **hand?**

I have the roots **man** and **manu.**
Who has the word that describes what you do when you make something by
hand or by machine that can be sold to someone?

I have the word **manufacture.**
Who has the word that names the person who has the upper **hand** in a business or
working environment and is sometimes called the "boss"?

I have the word **manager.**
Who has the word that names the **hand** treatment that some people enjoy getting?

I have the word **manicure.**
Who has the word that describes what you do to something when you carefully
move it around or change it by **hand?**

I have the word **manipulate.**
Who has the word that names the book that will tell you how to put something
together by **hand?**

I have the word **manual.**
Who has the word that names the **handcuffs** that are sometimes used in old movies?

I have the word **manacles.**
Who has the word that means that people are set free, such as with a historical proclamation?

I have the word **emancipate.**
Who has the word that describes how a car test driver weaves in and out of the
cones while checking the safety of a car on the road?

I have the word **maneuver.**
Who has the word that names an order that must be followed?

I have the word **mandate.**
Who has the word that names a **handwritten** document that is often the first draft
of a book or script?

I have the word **manuscript.**
Who has the first card?

Vocabulary Quiz: man, manu

Shade in the bubble for the correct word.

Ⓐ Ⓑ Ⓒ Ⓓ   **1.** If you are trying to get the key into your bike lock, but it's a bit rusted, then you'll have to do this carefully to the lock to get it to open.
A) manipulate   **B)** manacle   **C)** mandate   **D)** manufacture

Ⓐ Ⓑ Ⓒ Ⓓ   **2.** This comes with most products that you buy to tell you how to use them properly and/or set them up.
A) manacle   **B)** manicure   **C)** manager   **D)** manual

Ⓐ Ⓑ Ⓒ Ⓓ   **3.** The more expensive it is for the workers and the companies to do this, the higher the price you will have to pay for the product.
A) manipulate   **B)** manufacture   **C)** maneuver   **D)** emancipate

Ⓐ Ⓑ Ⓒ Ⓓ   **4.** Which word is the name of the treatment that makes the hands look fresh?
A) manicure   **B)** maneuver   **C)** emancipation   **D)** manacle

Ⓐ Ⓑ Ⓒ Ⓓ   **5.** Authors create these before they are edited and revised by their publishing companies.
A) manuals   **B)** manacles   **C)** manuscripts   **D)** maneuvers

Ⓐ Ⓑ Ⓒ Ⓓ   **6.** This person at Chicken Lickin' was in charge of hiring the new workers for the summer.
A) manacle   **B)** manager   **C)** emancipator   **D)** maneuver

Ⓐ Ⓑ Ⓒ Ⓓ   **7.** Old books sometimes use this word instead of the word *handcuffs*.
A) maneuvers   **B)** manacles   **C)** emancipate   **D)** mandates

Ⓐ Ⓑ Ⓒ Ⓓ   **8.** What does a town, city, state, or country create to make sure that a law is followed?
A) mandate   **B)** manipulate   **C)** maneuver   **D)** emancipate

Ⓐ Ⓑ Ⓒ Ⓓ   **9.** When the boy tried to ride his bike carefully around the cones, what did he do?
A) maneuver   **B)** manacles   **C)** manuals   **D)** mandates

Ⓐ Ⓑ Ⓒ Ⓓ   **10.** How do we describe a group of people who are set free from unfair laws or capture?
A) manacled   **B)** emancipated   **C)** maneuvered   **D)** manipulated

Write the correct word on the line so the sentence makes sense.

11. At the silent auction, the teacher offered to take the winning students to get _____ so their hands and nails would feel fresh and clean.

12. It was hard to _____ the new overalls, but the child finally got them to close.

13. The neighbors had to _____ around the fallen trees after the tornado touched down on their street.

14. The state of California _____ the use of bicycle helmets for safety reasons.

15. "May I please speak with your _____? My hamburger is cold!"

Greek and Latin Roots © 2004 Creative Teaching Press

Name _____   Date _____

Review Test: ped and man, manu

Shade in the bubble for the correct word.

Ⓐ Ⓑ Ⓒ Ⓓ   **1.** What are lions, wolves, and hares examples of?
     A) bipeds   **B)** tripods   **C)** quadrupeds   **D)** peddlers

Ⓐ Ⓑ Ⓒ Ⓓ   **2.** If someone was held captive and then set free, what happened to him?
     A) manacles   **B)** emancipation   **C)** pedicure   **D)** maneuvered

Ⓐ Ⓑ Ⓒ Ⓓ   **3.** What does a company do if they create sports sneakers and sell them?
     A) peddler   **B)** manipulate   **C)** maneuver   **D)** manufacture

Ⓐ Ⓑ Ⓒ Ⓓ   **4.** If someone comes knocking on your door trying to sell magazine subscriptions, what would you call him?
     A) pedestrian   **B)** impediment   **C)** manager   **D)** peddler

Ⓐ Ⓑ Ⓒ Ⓓ   **5.** What is a person doing when she tries to open the bike lock?
     A) manipulate   **B)** pedal   **C)** mandate   **D)** manuscript

Ⓐ Ⓑ Ⓒ Ⓓ   **6.** What do authors write?
     A) mandates   **B)** manuscripts   **C)** pedicures   **D)** maneuvers

Ⓐ Ⓑ Ⓒ Ⓓ   **7.** Who is the person in charge of other people in a company or restaurant?
     A) manager   **B)** peddler   **C)** pedestrian   **D)** manacle

Ⓐ Ⓑ Ⓒ Ⓓ   **8.** Watch out! There's a _____ crossing the street!
     A) millipede   **B)** pedestrian   **C)** mandate   **D)** manipulator

Ⓐ Ⓑ Ⓒ Ⓓ   **9.** Many people set goals and find little things standing in their way, but they never give up! What are the little things called?
     A) pedicures   **B)** manuals   **C)** bipeds   **D)** impediments

Ⓐ Ⓑ Ⓒ Ⓓ   **10.** What does the root **ped** mean?
     A) foot   **B)** hands   **C)** together   **D)** front

Ⓐ Ⓑ Ⓒ Ⓓ   **11.** What do the roots **man** and **manu** mean?
     A) foot   **B)** hand   **C)** together   **D)** to do

Ⓐ Ⓑ Ⓒ Ⓓ   ***12.** What does **tri** mean in the word *tripod*?
     A) hold   **B)** attempt   **C)** strong   **D)** three

Ⓐ Ⓑ Ⓒ Ⓓ   ***13.** What does **bi** mean in the word *biped*?
     A) three   **B)** four   **C)** two   **D)** strong

Ⓐ Ⓑ Ⓒ Ⓓ   **14.** manicure : _____ :: pedicure : _____
     A) feet, hands   **B)** over, under   **C)** hands, feet   **D)** dirty, clean

Ⓐ Ⓑ Ⓒ Ⓓ   **15.** On television commercials that advertise sporty cars, what do the drivers sometimes do around cones set up in a road?
     A) manipulate   **B)** maneuver   **C)** pedal   **D)** peddlers

Greek and Latin Roots © 2004 Creative Teaching Press

Word List: spec = see, look

Vocabulary	Definitions
circumspect (adj)	careful to **look** at all possibilities before acting; cautious; aware of consequences
inspect (v)	to **look** at carefully in search of flaws
introspection (n)	the act of **looking** into one's own thoughts and feelings
perspective (n)	one way of **looking** at things
respect (v)	to **look** up to someone; to show honor
retrospective (adj)	**looking** back at past things
spectacle (n)	something displayed for the public to **see**
spectacles (n)	glasses that help someone **see** better
spectator (n)	a person who **watches** something, such as a sporting event
speculate (v)	to **look** at and think about something from different points of view

Greek and Latin Roots © 2004 Creative Teaching Press

Vocabulary Sort: spec

inspect	to **look** up to someone; to show honor
speculate	to **look** at and think about something from different points of view
perspective	careful to **look** at all possibilities before acting; cautious; aware of consequences
spectacle	a person who **watches** something, such as a sporting event
introspection	**looking** back at past things
spectator	to **look** at carefully in search of flaws
circumspect	glasses that help someone **see** better
retrospective	the act of **looking** into your own thoughts and feelings
spectacles	something displayed for the public to **see**
respect	one way of **looking** at things

Greek and Latin Roots © 2004 Creative Teaching Press

Read-Around Review: spec

I have the first card.
Who has the root that means **look** or **see?**

I have the root **spec.**
Who has the word that describes what you do when you **look** at something carefully
to make sure there isn't anything wrong with it?

I have the word **inspect.**
Who has the word that describes what you show someone when you **look** up to them?

I have the word **respect.**
Who has the word that names the glasses that people wear to help them **see** better?

I have the word **spectacles.**
Who has the word that describes a person who **watches** something, such as a
pro basketball game?

I have the word **spectator.**
Who has the word that describes how you are being when you **look** back at past things
and think about the past?

I have the word **retrospective.**
Who has the word that describes a way of **looking** at things from one point of view?

I have the word **perspective.**
Who has the word that means **looking** at something from different points of view,
which requires more of an open mind?

I have the word **speculate.**
Who has the word that names what a child would be making out of herself if she threw
a fit in the middle of a crowded mall because she didn't get her way?

I have the word **spectacle.**
Who has the word that describes what a person is practicing when he **looks**
into his own thoughts and feelings?

I have the word **introspection.**
Who has the word that describes how a person might **look** if she is careful and **looks**
all around before doing something?

I have the word **circumspect.**
Who has the first card?

Greek and Latin Roots © 2004 Creative Teaching Press

Name _____   Date _____

Vocabulary Quiz: spec

Shade in the bubble for the correct word.

Ⓐ Ⓑ Ⓒ Ⓓ   **1.** If you ever cross the border into another country, then you will see the border control agents doing this to people and vehicles.
   A) spectacles   **B)** inspecting   **C)** retrospective   **D)** introspection

Ⓐ Ⓑ Ⓒ Ⓓ   **2.** These people at the baseball game organized a giant "wave."
   A) spectators   **B)** spectacles   **C)** perspectives   **D)** circumspect

Ⓐ Ⓑ Ⓒ Ⓓ   **3.** Sometimes it's hard to do this when you are involved in the situation.
   A) introspection   **B)** spectacle   **C)** circumspect   **D)** speculate

Ⓐ Ⓑ Ⓒ Ⓓ   **4.** The character in the story wore a pair of these to help him read the magic spells.
   A) retrospectives **B)** respect   **C)** perspectives   **D)** spectacles

Ⓐ Ⓑ Ⓒ Ⓓ   **5.** What should you always show to your parents?
   A) introspection   **B)** circumspection **C)** inspections   **D)** respect

Ⓐ Ⓑ Ⓒ Ⓓ   **6.** Your opinion on a decision without listening to others will probably only reflect your what?
   A) circumspect   **B)** inspection   **C)** perspective   **D)** spectacles

Ⓐ Ⓑ Ⓒ Ⓓ   **7.** What are you practicing when you think hard about why you are sad or happy?
   A) introspection   **B)** circumspection **C)** inspection   **D)** spectacles

Ⓐ Ⓑ Ⓒ Ⓓ   **8.** In the courtroom, the jury thinks before acting. How do we describe this?
   A) circumspect   **B)** introspect   **C)** retrospect   **D)** inspect

Ⓐ Ⓑ Ⓒ Ⓓ   **9.** This is also sometimes described by adults as "making a scene."
   A) spectacle   **B)** introspection   **C)** spectacles   **D)** spectators

Ⓐ Ⓑ Ⓒ Ⓓ   **10.** Sometimes when a famous actor dies, there is this type of tribute on television that takes a look back at all of the actor's movies.
   A) retrospective   **B)** introspection   **C)** circumspection   **D)** spectacle

Write the correct word on the line so the sentence makes sense.

11. The baby didn't mean to, but he made a _____ of himself when he threw his rattle across the quiet fancy restaurant.

12. The two-hour special feature was dedicated to pets around the world. It was a _____ documentary that looked back on how pets have been helping people for centuries.

13. Do you wear _____ to help you see better?

14. At the concert, you could hear the _____ singing along to every song with the band.

15. From your _____, who was the kindest character in the story?

Greek and Latin Roots © 2004 Creative Teaching Press

Word List: dict = speak

Vocabulary	Definitions
contradict (v)	to **speak** against; to **say** the opposite
dictation (n)	what is written down as someone **says** it
dictator (n)	a leader who **speaks** and rules with total power
diction (n)	the manner in which something is expressed in words (written or **spoken**)
dictionary (n)	a reference book in which **spoken** or written words are defined
dictum (n)	a judge's ruling or **statement**
edict (n)	public **words** issued by an official that explain a law or command
indictment (n)	formal words **spoken** or written by a jury that charge a person with a crime
predict (v)	to **say** what will happen before it occurs
verdict (n)	the decision a jury makes in a trial; the decision **said** by the jury

Greek and Latin Roots © 2004 Creative Teaching Press

Vocabulary Sort: dict

predict	to **speak** against; to **say** the opposite
dictator	the decision a jury makes in a trial; the decision **said** by the jury
indictment	a reference book in which **spoken** or written words are defined
dictum	the manner in which something is expressed in words (written or **spoken**)
dictation	public **words** issued by an official that explain a law or command
verdict	a leader who **speaks** and rules with total power
edict	formal words **spoken** or written by a jury that charge a person with a crime
diction	what is written down as someone **says** it
dictionary	a judge's ruling or **statement**
contradict	to **say** what will happen before it occurs

Greek and Latin Roots © 2004 Creative Teaching Press

Read-Around Review: dict

I have the first card.
Who has the root that means **speak?**

I have the root **dict.**
Who has the word that describes what someone writes down when he or she writes
down everything you **say** so that you can remember it later?

I have the word **dictation.**
Who has the word that describes how someone **speaks?**

I have the word **diction.**
Who has the word that names the book you would look in if you wanted to know
how to **say** a word correctly or if you needed a definition for a word?

I have the word **dictionary.**
Who has the word that names the act of officially charging someone with a crime?

I have the word **indictment.**
Who has the word that names a judge's ruling or **statement?**

I have the word **dictum.**
Who has the word that describes what someone does when she doesn't agree
and actually **says** the opposite as someone else?

I have the word **contradict.**
Who has the word that describes what good readers do before reading to help
them form expectations about what they will read?

I have the word **predict.**
Who has the word that describes what someone would have heard **announced**
many years ago in a town square, perhaps by a mayor?

I have the word **edict.**
Who has the word that names the type of ruler who makes everyone do what he or she **says?**

I have the word **dictator.**
Who has the word that names the decision a jury makes in a trial related to guilt or innocence?

I have the word **verdict.**
Who has the first card?

Greek and Latin Roots © 2004 Creative Teaching Press

Name _____   Date _____

Vocabulary Quiz: dict

Shade in the bubble for the correct word.

Ⓐ Ⓑ Ⓒ Ⓓ   **1.** The annual Horseracing Derby is coming up. Most people expect Solo's Shadow to come in first place. What are they making?
   A) verdicts   **B)** predictions   **C)** dictations   **D)** edicts

Ⓐ Ⓑ Ⓒ Ⓓ   **2.** All United States citizens are required by law to serve on a jury if asked to do so. If this happens to you, you will have to decide on what?
   A) dictionary   **B)** dictations   **C)** verdict   **D)** diction

Ⓐ Ⓑ Ⓒ Ⓓ   **3.** Some people seem to have an accent. They simply differ in what compared to you?
   A) dictation   **B)** indictments   **C)** edicts   **D)** diction

Ⓐ Ⓑ Ⓒ Ⓓ   **4.** Every library has a few of these to help people say words the right way and figure out what they mean.
   A) dictionaries   **B)** dictums   **C)** predictions   **D)** contradictions

Ⓐ Ⓑ Ⓒ Ⓓ   **5.** The usual result of this is a criminal trial to determine guilt or innocence.
   A) indictment   **B)** contradiction   **C)** dictation   **D)** edicts

Ⓐ Ⓑ Ⓒ Ⓓ   **6.** History tells of many of this type of person who ruled by force so that people had very little control over their own lives.
   A) dictum   **B)** edict   **C)** dictator   **D)** verdict

Ⓐ Ⓑ Ⓒ Ⓓ   **7.** If an official met with many people around him to announce why a certain law must be followed, what would he be saying?
   A) dictum   **B)** edict   **C)** dictation   **D)** contradiction

Ⓐ Ⓑ Ⓒ Ⓓ   **8.** A secretary records this on a notepad or computer for the boss, so that the boss will remember what he or she said exactly.
   A) dictation   **B)** edicts   **C)** predictions   **D)** dictums

Ⓐ Ⓑ Ⓒ Ⓓ   **9.** It is not polite to do this to your parents.
   A) contradict   **B)** predict   **C)** dictum   **D)** indictment

Ⓐ Ⓑ Ⓒ Ⓓ   **10.** The judge read this to the courtroom.
   A) dictionary   **B)** edict   **C)** prediction   **D)** dictum

Write the correct word on the line so the sentence makes sense.

11. What do you _____ will happen if you spend tomorrow's lunch money on a candy bar today?

12. If you lived in a country with a _____ as the leader, you would be told what you could and could not do.

13. The _____ means that the man will face a trial to decide if he committed the crime.

14. If you want to know how to say the word *indictment* properly, then you could look in the _____.

15. The way that you speak is called your _____.

Greek and Latin Roots © 2004 Creative Teaching Press

Name _____   Date _____

Review Test: spec and dict

Shade in the bubble for the correct word.

Ⓐ Ⓑ Ⓒ Ⓓ   **1.** What would you call a person who looks at clothing that comes off of the assembly line to check that it was made properly?
A) dictum   **B)** dictator   **C)** indictment   **D)** inspector

Ⓐ Ⓑ Ⓒ Ⓓ   **2.** There were so many of these at the basketball championship that the arena was sold out!
A) dictators   **B)** predictions   **C)** spectators   **D)** inspectors

Ⓐ Ⓑ Ⓒ Ⓓ   **3.** The man on trial was waiting to hear what the jury would decide. What was he waiting for the jury to give?
A) dictation   **B)** verdict   **C)** introspection   **D)** dictation

Ⓐ Ⓑ Ⓒ Ⓓ   **4.** You do this when you consider what your parents would think in addition to what you think you should do.
A) perspective   **B)** speculate   **C)** retrospect   **D)** circumspect

Ⓐ Ⓑ Ⓒ Ⓓ   **5.** This decision that a person should be tried on criminal charges is called what?
A) indictment   **B)** dictation   **C)** dictum   **D)** dictate

Ⓐ Ⓑ Ⓒ Ⓓ   **6.** What do people with good character show to other people?
A) circumspection   **B)** dictionaries   **C)** spectacles   **D)** respect

Ⓐ Ⓑ Ⓒ Ⓓ   **7.** What are the historical rulers who forced everyone to follow their laws and wishes called?
A) indictments   **B)** dictums   **C)** dictators   **D)** spectacles

Ⓐ Ⓑ Ⓒ Ⓓ   **8.** What do eye doctors make for people with vision problems?
A) edicts   **B)** perspectives   **C)** predictions   **D)** spectacles

Ⓐ Ⓑ Ⓒ Ⓓ   **9.** If you do this to a person in authority in a rude voice, then you will probably be punished.
A) contradict   **B)** dictate   **C)** retrospeculate   **D)** predict

Ⓐ Ⓑ Ⓒ Ⓓ   **10.** What does the root **spec** mean?
A) look   **B)** say   **C)** help   **D)** show

Ⓐ Ⓑ Ⓒ Ⓓ   **11.** What does the root **dict** mean?
A) look   **B)** speak   **C)** help   **D)** show

Ⓐ Ⓑ Ⓒ Ⓓ   *__12.__ What does **circum** mean in the word *circumspect*?
A) together   **B)** look   **C)** write   **D)** around

Ⓐ Ⓑ Ⓒ Ⓓ   *__13.__ What does **pre** mean in the word *predict*?
A) after   **B)** before   **C)** together   **D)** say

Ⓐ Ⓑ Ⓒ Ⓓ   *__14.__ What does **contra** most likely mean in the word *contradict*?
A) together   **B)** within   **C)** against   **D)** outside

Ⓐ Ⓑ Ⓒ Ⓓ   *__15.__ What does the suffix- **or** most likely mean in the words *inspector* and *dictator*?
A) in the direction of   **B)** a person who   **C)** similar to   **D)** able to

Greek and Latin Roots © 2004 Creative Teaching Press

Word List: ject = throw

Vocabulary	Definitions
dejected (adj)	to feel sad; to feel **thrown** down in spirit
eject (v)	to **throw** out
injection (n)	a shot; the **"throwing"** of medicine into the body by a needle
interjection (n)	a word **thrown** into a sentence or conversation
jettison (v)	to **throw** goods overboard to lighten the load on a boat or an airplane
projectile (n)	an object **thrown** into the air with great force
projector (n)	a machine that **throws** an image onto a wall
reject (v)	to **throw** something out because it's defective and can't be used again
subject (v)	to **throw** oneself under someone else's rule
trajectory (n)	the curved path of an object **thrown** into space

Greek and Latin Roots © 2004 Creative Teaching Press

Vocabulary Sort: ject

eject	the curved path of an object **thrown** into space
projector	to **throw** something out because it's defective and can't be used again
projectile	to **throw** goods overboard to lighten the load on a boat or an airplane
dejected	to feel sad; to feel **thrown** down in spirit
subject	a machine that **throws** an image onto a wall
jettison	to **throw** out
trajectory	a shot; the **"throwing"** of medicine into the body by a needle
injection	an object **thrown** into the air with great force
interjection	a word **thrown** into a sentence or conversation
reject	to **throw** oneself under someone else's rule

Greek and Latin Roots © 2004 Creative Teaching Press

Read-Around Review: ject

I have the first card.
Who has the root that means **throw?**

I have the root **ject.**
Who has the word that describes what you do to something when it can't
be used again or it's rotten?

I have the word **reject.**
Who has the word that describes how you are feeling when you are very sad?

I have the word **dejected.**
Who has the word that names the word that is **thrown** into a sentence or conversation?

I have the word **interjection.**
Who has the word that describes what people must do to themselves when
they work for someone else?

I have the word **subject.**
Who has the word that names what you would be getting if the doctor gave you a flu shot?

I have the word **injection.**
Who has the word that names the machine that makes images appear on the wall?

I have the word **projector.**
Who has the word that names the curved path that your paper airplane would have
as it goes up and down in the air after you **threw** it?

I have the word **trajectory.**
Who has the word that names what is done when goods are **thrown** overboard
to lighten a boat's load?

I have the word **jettison.**
Who has the word that describes what you do when you **throw** something out?

I have the word **eject.**
Who has the word that names what you could call on object that is **thrown**
into the air with great force?

I have the word **projectile.**
Who has the first card?

Greek and Latin Roots © 2004 Creative Teaching Press

Name _____ Date _____

Vocabulary Quiz: ject

Shade in the bubble for the correct word.

Ⓐ Ⓑ Ⓒ Ⓓ 1. This is what happened to the basketball player when he got his sixth foul.
   A) projectile   **B)** ejected   **C)** injected   **D)** jettison

Ⓐ Ⓑ Ⓒ Ⓓ 2. A doctor gives these to his patients to help them feel better.
   A) rejections   **B)** injections   **C)** projectors   **D)** interjections

Ⓐ Ⓑ Ⓒ Ⓓ 3. Tom and Keith are talking about their vacation to the valley. Dave comes up and says,
   "Aha! I knew you were going there!" What did Dave add to the conversation?
   A) jettison   **B)** trajectory   **C)** projectiles   **D)** interjection

Ⓐ Ⓑ Ⓒ Ⓓ 4. Danielle was so competitive that she always felt like this when her water polo team lost.
   A) jettison   **B)** subjected   **C)** rejected   **D)** dejected

Ⓐ Ⓑ Ⓒ Ⓓ 5. "Ahoy there mates! We need to throw this overboard!" What will the fishermen do to some
   of their cargo?
   A) jettison   **B)** subject   **C)** projectile   **D)** reject

Ⓐ Ⓑ Ⓒ Ⓓ 6. Mr. Nguyen said, "Who threw that eraser across the desk? It could have knocked me over!"
   What was the eraser?
   A) projectile   **B)** trajectory   **C)** jettison   **D)** injection

Ⓐ Ⓑ Ⓒ Ⓓ 7. This machine makes things look bigger on the wall so everyone in the classroom can see
   the writing.
   A) projectile   **B)** projector   **C)** trajectory   **D)** subject

Ⓐ Ⓑ Ⓒ Ⓓ 8. The higher the paper airplane goes, the wider the angle of which of the following?
   A) rejection   **B)** projectile   **C)** trajectory   **D)** subject

Ⓐ Ⓑ Ⓒ Ⓓ 9. At home, you are this to your parents' rules and expectations.
   A) rejected   **B)** injected   **C)** jettison   **D)** subjected

Ⓐ Ⓑ Ⓒ Ⓓ 10. The Boston Button Factory only produces buttons with straight sides. What will it do to all
   circular buttons?
   A) reject   **B)** subject   **C)** interject   **D)** projectile

Write the correct word on the line so the sentence makes sense.

11. The American colonists were _____ to British rule until they won the American Revolution.

12. If someone yells "Hey!" in the middle of your conversation, the type of comment is an _____.

13. Is the _____ plugged in? The wall is still bare.

14. If the _____ is sharp, then it could hurt someone when it comes down.

15. Brenton hardly ever feels _____ because he has an easygoing attitude and always looks
    on the bright side of things.

Greek and Latin Roots © 2004 Creative Teaching Press

Word List: sect = cut; separate

Vocabulary	Definitions
bisect (v)	to **cut** into two pieces
dissect (v)	to **cut** apart for the purpose of investigation
insect (n)	a class of small arthropod animals that has three **separate** sections to their bodies: head, thorax, abdomen
intersection (n)	the point at which two lines or roads meet and **cut** across each other
section (n)	a **separate** part of something
sectional (n)	a couch that is made up of **separate** pieces
sector (n)	a **separate** part of a society, group, or area
transect (v)	to **cut** across something
trisect (v)	to **cut** into three **separate** pieces
vivisection (n)	surgery on living animals; medical research that involves **cutting** into living animals to study organs, tissues, or diseases

Greek and Latin Roots © 2004 Creative Teaching Press

Vocabulary Sort: sect

intersection	to **cut** across something
trisect	a **separate** part of something
dissect	a **separate** part of a society, group, or area
section	to **cut** into three **separate** pieces
transect	a class of small arthropod animals that has three **separate** sections to their bodies: head, thorax, abdomen
vivisection	a couch that is made up of **separate** pieces
insect	to **cut** into two pieces
sectional	surgery on living animals; medical research that involves **cutting** into living animals to study organs, tissues, or diseases
sector	to **cut** apart for the purpose of investigation
bisect	the point at which two lines or roads meet and **cut** across each other

Greek and Latin Roots © 2004 Creative Teaching Press

Read-Around Review: sect

I have the first card.
Who has the root that means **cut** or **separate?**

I have the root **sect.**
Who has the word that describes what you would do if you **cut** something into three sections?

I have the word **trisect.**
Who has the word that names the small class of arthropods that have
three sections to their bodies?

I have the word **insects.**
Who has the word that names the part on a map at which two streets cross each other?

I have the word **intersection.**
Who has the word that describes what you would do to something if you **cut** it into two pieces?

I have the word **bisect.**
Who has the word that names a **separate** part of a society or group?

I have the word **sector.**
Who has the word that identifies the surgery that is done on living animals for medical research?

I have the word **vivisection.**
Who has the word that names a type of couch that is made up of several pieces?

I have the word **sectional.**
Who has the word that describes what you would do if you **cut** across something?

I have the word **transect.**
Who has the word that describes a **separate** part of something?

I have the word **section.**
Who has the word that means to **cut** something apart so that it can be investigated?

I have the word **dissect.**
Who has the first card?

Greek and Latin Roots © 2004 Creative Teaching Press

Name _____   Date _____

Vocabulary Quiz: sect

Shade in the bubble for the correct word.

Ⓐ Ⓑ Ⓒ Ⓓ   **1.** This is what a student would do if he were to investigate the inside of a squid for a science class.
    A) section   **B)** dissect   **C)** sectional   **D)** insect

Ⓐ Ⓑ Ⓒ Ⓓ   **2.** What would you call a fly since it has a head, an abdomen, and a thorax?
    A) insect   **B)** sector   **C)** sectional   **D)** intersection

Ⓐ Ⓑ Ⓒ Ⓓ   **3.** What do you call a section of the business world that produces clothing?
    A) sector   **B)** transect   **C)** intersection   **D)** sectional

Ⓐ Ⓑ Ⓒ Ⓓ   **4.** There is often a street light on this part of the road for safety reasons.
    A) intersection   **B)** sectional   **C)** vivisection   **D)** sector

Ⓐ Ⓑ Ⓒ Ⓓ   **5.** Scientist Schmitz is researching cancer treatments with the help of animals. What does he likely perform?
    A) intersection   **B)** sectional   **C)** bisecting   **D)** vivisection

Ⓐ Ⓑ Ⓒ Ⓓ   **6.** A chapter of a book can be called one of these compared to the whole book.
    A) vivisection   **B)** sectional   **C)** section   **D)** transect

Ⓐ Ⓑ Ⓒ Ⓓ   **7.** When building a new road, a special blade is used to cut across the cement. What will this blade do?
    A) transect   **B)** vivisection   **C)** intersection   **D)** sector

Ⓐ Ⓑ Ⓒ Ⓓ   **8.** Sometimes in science investigations, you'll be asked to investigate a species by cutting it in three separate pieces. What will you do?
    A) bisect   **B)** quadrisect   **C)** trisect   **D)** dissect

Ⓐ Ⓑ Ⓒ Ⓓ   **9.** Mr. Guzman hopes to put a huge one of these in his new living room.
    A) dissection   **B)** sectional   **C)** sector   **D)** intersection

Ⓐ Ⓑ Ⓒ Ⓓ   **10.** Did you already cut your soft cookie into two pieces to share with me? What did you do?
    A) trisect   **B)** dissect   **C)** quadrisect   **D)** bisect

Write the correct word on the line so the sentence makes sense.

11. Callie the Cat likes to sleep on the middle section of the _____ in the living room.

12. The city named the _____ Colby's Crossing after the man who started the first mill in the town right where the two roads cross today.

13. Paolo ordered an avocado roll from the sushi restaurant. While watching, he noticed that the sushi chef cut across it to _____ the avocado roll.

14. There is a _____ of the population who still don't believe in using electricity or other modern conveniences.

15. Put the following words in order according to how many cuts would be made. (fewest to most)
quadrisect   bisect   trisect   _____

Greek and Latin Roots © 2004 Creative Teaching Press

Name _____   Date _____

Review Test: ject and sect

Shade in the bubble for the correct word.

Ⓐ Ⓑ Ⓒ Ⓓ   **1.** What will you get to do in science class one day if you haven't already had a chance to do it to investigate the insides of creatures?
A) project   **B)** sector   **C)** inject   **D)** dissect

Ⓐ Ⓑ Ⓒ Ⓓ   **2.** What can pilots do if something goes wrong with their aircraft?
A) interject   **B)** eject   **C)** transect   **D)** bisect

Ⓐ Ⓑ Ⓒ Ⓓ   **3.** What is the method used by doctors to put liquid medicine into your blood stream quickly to make you feel better?
A) injection   **B)** dissection   **C)** vivisection   **D)** jettison

Ⓐ Ⓑ Ⓒ Ⓓ   **4.** In the days of the kings and queens, most people were _____ to the laws and rules the royalty created.
A) subjected   **B)** trisected   **C)** rejected   **D)** insected

Ⓐ Ⓑ Ⓒ Ⓓ   **5.** What is the area where two roads cross called?
A) dissection   **B)** intersection   **C)** vivisection   **D)** jettison

Ⓐ Ⓑ Ⓒ Ⓓ   **6.** How might a child feel if he just found out that his goldfish died?
A) sectional   **B)** transected   **C)** rejected   **D)** dejected

Ⓐ Ⓑ Ⓒ Ⓓ   **7.** A comment someone throws into your conversation when you didn't ask for it is called what?
A) injection   **B)** interjection   **C)** transector   **D)** projectile

Ⓐ Ⓑ Ⓒ Ⓓ   **8.** If you only want to eat half of your beef jerky, then you might do this to it.
A) trisect   **B)** intersect   **C)** reject   **D)** bisect

Ⓐ Ⓑ Ⓒ Ⓓ   **9.** You can buy one of these at a furniture store and it can be changed into different positions to fit the room.
A) jettison   **B)** vivisection   **C)** sectional   **D)** projector

Ⓐ Ⓑ Ⓒ Ⓓ   **10.** What does the root **sect** mean?
A) under   **B)** throw   **C)** cut   **D)** across

Ⓐ Ⓑ Ⓒ Ⓓ   **11.** What does the root **ject** mean?
A) under   **B)** throw   **C)** cut   **D)** across

Ⓐ Ⓑ Ⓒ Ⓓ   ***12.** What does **trans** mean in the word *transect*?
A) half   **B)** two   **C)** three   **D)** across

Ⓐ Ⓑ Ⓒ Ⓓ   ***13.** What does **re** mean in the word *reject*?
A) again   **B)** within   **C)** after   **D)** outside

Ⓐ Ⓑ Ⓒ Ⓓ   ***14.** What does **viv** most likely mean in the word *vivisection*?
A) cut   **B)** life   **C)** path   **D)** writing

Ⓐ Ⓑ Ⓒ Ⓓ   **15.** If you were going to dissect an insect, which would be the most logical way?
A) transect   **B)** trisect   **C)** bisect   **D)** sectional

Greek and Latin Roots © 2004 Creative Teaching Press

Word List: port = carry

Vocabulary	Definitions
deport (v)	to **carry** or send away from a country; to banish
export (v)	to **carry** out of the country
import (v)	to **carry** into the country
portable (adj)	capable of being easily **carried**
portage (n)	the route over which boats and supplies are **carried** overland from one lake or river to another
porter (n)	an attendant who **carries** travelers' luggage for them
portfolio (n)	a case for **carrying** loose papers
report (n)	a collection of writing that **carries** information to be shared again with someone new
support (v)	to **carry** the weight of something
transport (v)	to **carry** something from one place to another

Greek and Latin Roots © 2004 Creative Teaching Press

Vocabulary Sort: port

transport	to **carry** out of the country
import	a case for **carrying** loose papers
porter	an attendant who **carries** travelers' luggage for them
report	to **carry** or send away from a country; to banish
support	a collection of writing that **carries** information to be shared again with someone new
portage	the route over which boats and supplies are **carried** overland from one lake or river to another
deport	capable of being easily **carried**
portfolio	to **carry** the weight of something
portable	to **carry** into the country
export	to **carry** something from one place to another

Greek and Latin Roots © 2004 Creative Teaching Press

Read-Around Review: port

I have the first card.
Who has the root that means **carry?**

I have the root **port.**
Who has the word that describes what you do when you **carry** the weight of something such as a baby so that it doesn't fall?

I have the word **support.**
Who has the word that describes what companies do when they sell goods outside of the United States and ship them to other countries?

I have the word **export.**
Who has the word that names the person who will **carry** your bags to your room in a hotel if they are heavy or if you're too tired?

I have the word **porter.**
Who has the word that describes anything that can be easily **carried** from one place to another such as a laptop computer or a DVD player that fits in your hand?

I have the word **portable.**
Who has the word that describes what people do when they move things from one location to another?

I have the word **transport.**
Who has the word that names the case that **carries** loose papers and often artwork so that it's not destroyed while traveling?

I have the word **portfolio.**
Who has the word that names the overland route over which boats and supplies are **carried** from one lake or river to another?

I have the word **portage.**
Who has the word that names the collection of writing that **carries** information and usually teaches the reader something about a specific subject?

I have the word **report.**
Who has the word that describes what might happen to someone if he or she is in the United States illegally?

I have the word **deported.**
Who has the word that describes what some companies do in the United States when it is cheaper for them to get their supplies from other countries?

I have the word **import.**
Who has the first card?

Greek and Latin Roots © 2004 Creative Teaching Press

Name _____   Date _____

Vocabulary Quiz: port

Shade in the bubble for the correct word.

Ⓐ Ⓑ Ⓒ Ⓓ **1.** If a country does not have a particular item, they may do this to get the item into their country.
A) export   B) report   C) support   D) import

Ⓐ Ⓑ Ⓒ Ⓓ **2.** A CD player that you can carry around with you is called this.
A) portfolio   B) portable   C) transport   D) portage

Ⓐ Ⓑ Ⓒ Ⓓ **3.** "Good morning, class. Today we will begin writing the facts that will share information with everyone about the different animals that live in Australia." What will the children write?
A) reports   B) deports   C) portfolios   D) exports

Ⓐ Ⓑ Ⓒ Ⓓ **4.** A pedestal that allows the heavy marble statue to be on display at the museum does which of the following for the statue?
A) reports   B) supports   C) exports   D) imports

Ⓐ Ⓑ Ⓒ Ⓓ **5.** "Thank you, Marco, for carrying all of my bags so far!" What is Marco's job?
A) portfolio   B) porter   C) exporter   D) deporter

Ⓐ Ⓑ Ⓒ Ⓓ **6.** A country that produces more of a supply than it needs will often do this with the product to make money.
A) export   B) import   C) support   D) deport

Ⓐ Ⓑ Ⓒ Ⓓ **7.** An artist usually carries his or her original sketches on a job interview in one of these.
A) portage   B) report   C) importer   D) portfolio

Ⓐ Ⓑ Ⓒ Ⓓ **8.** What do buses, trains, and other vehicles do to people?
A) import   B) deport   C) transport   D) export

Ⓐ Ⓑ Ⓒ Ⓓ **9.** Unfortunately, there are people who will be _____ if they are in the United States illegally.
A) portage   B) deported   C) imported   D) exported

Ⓐ Ⓑ Ⓒ Ⓓ **10.** The boat was moved from one lake to another over this.
A) export   B) portfolio   C) portage   D) deport

Write the correct word on the line so the sentence makes sense.

11. The state of Florida makes so many oranges that it _____ some to other states.

12. The state of Arizona _____ maple syrup from the state of Vermont.

13. Someday, there may be a _____ laptop computer for every student at school.

14. It is polite to tip the _____ for carrying your luggage to your room.

15. How will we ever _____ this huge bed to the other side of the country when we move?

Greek and Latin Roots © 2004 Creative Teaching Press

Word List: miss, mit = send

Vocabulary	Definitions
admit (v)	to **send** someone in; to allow someone to enter
dismiss (v)	to **send** someone out; to let someone leave
emit (v)	to **send** out or give off (such as an odor)
intermission (n)	a break between acts of a play or performance during which people are **sent** out for snacks or stretch breaks
missile (n)	a weapon designed to be **sent** in the direction of a target
mission (n)	a special duty or function which a person or group is **sent** out to do
omit (v)	to leave out; to not **send**
remit (v)	to **send** back (usually related to paying bills)
submit (v)	to **"send"** yourself under someone else's control; to give in to someone else's power
transmit (v)	to **send** something across places; to pass along

Greek and Latin Roots © 2004 Creative Teaching Press

Vocabulary Sort: miss, mit

transmit	to leave out; to not **send**
intermission	to **send** someone out; to let someone leave
mission	to **"send"** yourself under someone else's control; to give in to someone else's power
dismiss	to **send** out or give off (such as an odor)
submit	a special duty or function which a person or group is **sent** out to do
remit	to **send** someone in; to allow someone to enter
emit	a weapon designed to be **sent** in the direction of a target
missile	a break between acts of a play or performance during which people are **sent** out for snacks or stretch breaks
omit	to **send** back (usually related to paying bills)
admit	to **send** something across places; to pass along

Greek and Latin Roots © 2004 Creative Teaching Press

Read-Around Review: miss, mit

I have the first card.
Who has the roots that mean **send?**

I have the roots **miss** and **mit.**
Who has the word that names the break between acts in a play or performance that **sends** people out into the lobby for some fresh air and stretching time?

I have the word **intermission.**
Who has the word that describes what you do when you **send** something across a wire, such as a television broadcast?

I have the word **transmit.**
Who has the word that describes what you do when you leave something out?

I have the word **omit.**
Who has the word that names a task that includes a special purpose?

I have the word **mission.**
Who has the word that describes what you do when you **send** someone out?

I have the word **dismiss.**
Who has the word that names the military weapon that is **sent** after a specific target?

I have the word **missile.**
Who has the word that describes what an odor might do from a rotten piece of fruit?

I have the word **emit.**
Who has the word that describes what adults have to do when they receive bills in the mail?

I have the word **remit.**
Who has the word that describes what someone does when he lets you into a private room?

I have the word **admit.**
Who has the word that describes what you must do to your parents' control or the school rules?

I have the word **submit.**
Who has the first card?

Greek and Latin Roots © 2004 Creative Teaching Press

Vocabulary Quiz: miss, mit

Shade in the bubble for the correct word.

Ⓐ Ⓑ Ⓒ Ⓓ   **1.** This is what your teacher does to you when it is time for recess and you are ready to go.
A) remit   **B)** submit   **C)** omit   **D)** dismiss

Ⓐ Ⓑ Ⓒ Ⓓ   **2.** You will notice that trash cans are good at doing this with odors.
A) omit   **B)** admit   **C)** emit   **D)** submit

Ⓐ Ⓑ Ⓒ Ⓓ   **3.** What do you call the break in a performance of any kind that allows you to go out to stretch?
A) intermission   **B)** transmit   **C)** mission   **D)** admission

Ⓐ Ⓑ Ⓒ Ⓓ   **4.** Which word identifies a weapon that is sent out to an enemy target?
A) mission   **B)** missile   **C)** admit   **D)** emit

Ⓐ Ⓑ Ⓒ Ⓓ   **5.** When you have to send something back, especially money for something that you bought, what do you do with the money?
A) remit   **B)** admit   **C)** dismiss   **D)** submit

Ⓐ Ⓑ Ⓒ Ⓓ   **6.** "Your writing is good, but you need to take out all of the *likes* that you have overused," said Ms. Jackson. What does the teacher want the student to do to the word *like*?
A) emit   **B)** omit   **C)** submit   **D)** admit

Ⓐ Ⓑ Ⓒ Ⓓ   **7.** This word describes what astronauts go on in search of scientific information on other planets and in space.
A) missile   **B)** admission   **C)** mission   **D)** dismissed

Ⓐ Ⓑ Ⓒ Ⓓ   **8.** When caught doing something wrong, a smart person will do this to authority.
A) submit   **B)** admit   **C)** omit   **D)** emit

Ⓐ Ⓑ Ⓒ Ⓓ   **9.** At private club meetings, there is often someone guarding the door to only allow certain people on a list inside. He will do what to the listed people?
A) submit   **B)** omit   **C)** emit   **D)** admit

Ⓐ Ⓑ Ⓒ Ⓓ   **10.** You can send messages around the world using e-mail on the Internet. It's one way of doing what to information?
A) transmitting   **B)** admitting   **C)** remitting   **D)** omitting

Write the correct word on the line so the sentence makes sense.

11. The movie theater tickets said " _____ One" on the front of each one.

12. If a bill is late, it will often say "Please _____ immediately."

13. Certain flowers _____ a pleasant odor, while others _____ a very bad smell.

14. My story was getting too long, so I had to _____ a part of it.

15. During _____, the lines at the popcorn stand were very long!

Greek and Latin Roots © 2004 Creative Teaching Press

Review Test: port and miss, mit

Shade in the bubble for the correct word.

Ⓐ Ⓑ Ⓒ Ⓓ   **1.** If you are sent out to do something special, what might that be called?
   A) missile   **B)** mission   **C)** export   **D)** portfolio

Ⓐ Ⓑ Ⓒ Ⓓ   **2.** In these busy days of moving around and working hard, what feature of products do adults love?
   A) submit   **B)** portable   **C)** imports   **D)** intermissions

Ⓐ Ⓑ Ⓒ Ⓓ   **3.** When someone says, "You can go now," what did she just do?
   A) imported   **B)** admitted   **C)** reported   **D)** dismissed

Ⓐ Ⓑ Ⓒ Ⓓ   **4.** Who would be willing to help you carry your bags up to your hotel room on vacation besides your parents?
   A) porter   **B)** portage   **C)** reporter   **D)** transitter

Ⓐ Ⓑ Ⓒ Ⓓ   **5.** Cargo ships and giant trucks are often used to do this to products from one place to another.
   A) import   **B)** transport   **C)** emit   **D)** admit

Ⓐ Ⓑ Ⓒ Ⓓ   **6.** When you need to send something in right away, what do you need to do to it?
   A) admit   **B)** export   **C)** remit   **D)** omit

Ⓐ Ⓑ Ⓒ Ⓓ   **7.** When you write one of these, you are telling the reader important information.
   A) report   **B)** support   **C)** portfolio   **D)** portage

Ⓐ Ⓑ Ⓒ Ⓓ   **8.** This is what you do if you leave something out.
   A) admit   **B)** remit   **C)** omit   **D)** import

Ⓐ Ⓑ Ⓒ Ⓓ   **9.** People need to do this to leaders of a nation, since they are in charge.
   A) remit   **B)** portage   **C)** export   **D)** submit

Ⓐ Ⓑ Ⓒ Ⓓ   **10.** What do the roots **mis** and **mit** mean?
   A) to throw   **B)** to send   **C)** to cut   **D)** to carry

Ⓐ Ⓑ Ⓒ Ⓓ   **11.** What does the root **port** mean?
   A) to carry   **B)** to throw   **C)** to cut   **D)** to toss

Ⓐ Ⓑ Ⓒ Ⓓ   ***12.** What does **trans** mean in the word *transmit*?
   A) half   **B)** two   **C)** three   **D)** across

Ⓐ Ⓑ Ⓒ Ⓓ   ***13.** What does **inter** mean in the word *intermission*?
   A) between   **B)** under   **C)** over   **D)** across

Ⓐ Ⓑ Ⓒ Ⓓ   ***14.** What does **tele** most likely mean in the word *telephone*?
   A) in   **B)** distance   **C)** apart   **D)** across

Ⓐ Ⓑ Ⓒ Ⓓ   **15.** into the country : _____ :: out of the country : _____
   A) deport, export   **B)** import, deport   **C)** export, import   **D)** import, export

Greek and Latin Roots © 2004 Creative Teaching Press

Word List: graph = writing

Vocabulary	Definitions
autobiography (n)	**writing** about a person's life **written** by that person
autograph (n)	the **writing** of one's own name
bibliography (n)	the **written** list of all the books used in a report or book
biography (n)	a book **written** about a person's life
cartography (n)	mapmaking; the **writing** involved in making maps or charts
homograph (n)	a word **written** the same way as another word but having a different meaning (e.g., bow—hair and bow—ship)
paragraph (n)	a section of **writing** that has a topic and concluding sentence
phonograph (n)	record player; a device that turns the **writing** on records into sound
photography (n)	the use of light to **record** an image using a camera
seismograph (n)	a device that **writes** down (records) the movements of the earth

Greek and Latin Roots © 2004 Creative Teaching Press

Vocabulary Sort: graph

autograph	a device that **writes** down (records) the movements of the earth
biography	the use of light to **record** an image using a camera
paragraph	the **written** list of all the books used in a report or book
seismograph	the **writing** of one's own name
photography	mapmaking; the **writing** involved in making maps or charts
autobiography	a book **written** about a person's life
homograph	record player; a device that turns the **writing** on records into sound
phonograph	a word **written** the same way as another word but having a different meaning (e.g., bow—hair and bow—ship)
bibliography	a section of **writing** that has a topic and concluding sentence
cartography	**writing** about a person's life **written** by that person

Greek and Latin Roots © 2004 Creative Teaching Press

Read-Around Review: graph

I have the first card.
Who has the root that means **writing?**

I have the root **graph.**
Who has the word that names the part of a piece of **writing** that begins with a topic sentence, describes the topic in detail, then ends with a concluding sentence?

I have the word **paragraph.**
Who has the word that names the type of book that was **written** about a person's life but was **written** by a different person than the subject of the book?

I have the word **biography.**
Who has the word that names the device that scientists who study earthquakes will look at when they want to know how strong an earthquake was?

I have the word **seismograph.**
Who has the word that names the science of mapmaking?

I have the word **cartography.**
Who has the word that names the machine that turns the **writing** on plastic disks (records) into music that you can hear?

I have the word **phonograph.**
Who has the word that names what someone has **written** when he or she has signed his or her own name on something?

I have the word **autograph.**
Who has the word that names the hobby or study of how light **records** an image using a camera?

I have the word **photography.**
Who has the word that names the type of book that is about a person's life and was **written** by that actual person?

I have the word **autobiography.**
Who has the word that labels two words that are spelled the same but usually have different meanings based on how you say them?

I have the word **homograph.**
Who has the word that names the page at the end of a book report that tells the reader which books were studied to create the piece of **writing?**

I have the word **bibliography.**
Who has the first card?

Greek and Latin Roots © 2004 Creative Teaching Press

Name _____ Date _____

Vocabulary Quiz: graph

Shade in the bubble for the correct word.

Ⓐ Ⓑ Ⓒ Ⓓ   **1.** What do fans of famous authors, artists, and actors like to ask for?
  A) biographies   **B)** autographs   **C)** phonographs   **D)** paragraphs

Ⓐ Ⓑ Ⓒ Ⓓ   **2.** What do you call a book about a person's life written by someone else?
  A) autobiography   **B)** autograph   **C)** biography   **D)** bibliography

Ⓐ Ⓑ Ⓒ Ⓓ   **3.** The National Geographic magazine hired many experts in this area to create its many excellent maps.
  A) seismography   **B)** bibliography   **C)** cartography   **D)** homography

Ⓐ Ⓑ Ⓒ Ⓓ   **4.** What is another name for a record player?
  A) bibliography   **B)** phonograph   **C)** recordgraph   **D)** homograph

Ⓐ Ⓑ Ⓒ Ⓓ   **5.** Which is a recording of images using light?
  A) phonograph   **B)** homograph   **C)** autograph   **D)** photograph

Ⓐ Ⓑ Ⓒ Ⓓ   **6.** What is the name of the device that tells scientists when an earthquake has occurred?
  A) seismograph   **B)** geograph   **C)** homograph   **D)** autograph

Ⓐ Ⓑ Ⓒ Ⓓ   **7.** What are many types of writing broken up into so that it makes sense and sounds clear?
  A) seismographs   **B)** autographs   **C)** bibliography   **D)** paragraphs

Ⓐ Ⓑ Ⓒ Ⓓ   **8.** If you are writing a report, this should be your last page.
  A) autograph   **B)** bibliography   **C)** autobiography   **D)** homograph

Ⓐ Ⓑ Ⓒ Ⓓ   **9.** First Lady Hillary Rodham Clinton wrote one of these about her life as wife of a United States president.
  A) biography   **B)** seismograph   **C)** autobiography   **D)** autograph

Ⓐ Ⓑ Ⓒ Ⓓ   **10.** A *bow* in your hair and the *bow* of a ship are called what type of words?
  A) homographs   **B)** autographs   **C)** seismographs   **D)** homophones

Write the correct word on the line so the sentence makes sense.

11. Many famous people today have written _____ about their own lives.

12. It's popular to go to an author signing to get an author's _____ on a book.

13. If you like to read and draw maps, perhaps you will study _____ in college.

14. If you are interested in how the earth sometimes moves, then one day you may learn how to operate a _____.

15. If you wrote a book about your teacher's life, it would be a _____.

Greek and Latin Roots © 2004 Creative Teaching Press

Word List: scrib, script = write

Vocabulary	Definitions
describe (v)	to say or **write** down how something or someone looks; to use adjectives in **writing**
inscription (n)	a short dedication **written** in a book or engraved on something, such as a coin or monument
manuscript (n)	a piece of **writing;** a book
postscript (n)	P.S.; a short bit of **writing** added after a letter is finished
prescription (n)	a piece of paper **written** by a doctor that lets you get medicine at the pharmacy
scribble (n)	sloppy **writing** that is hard to read
scribe (n)	a person who **writes** things down
script (n)	a set of papers with **writing** that will be read and acted out
subscription (n)	a **written** agreement to buy and read a magazine or newspaper for a set period of time
transcribe (v)	to **write** down or record; to translate

Vocabulary Sort: scrib, script

manuscript	to **write** down or record; to translate
postscript	a piece of paper **written** by a doctor that lets you get medicine at the pharmacy
subscription	a person who **writes** things down
script	sloppy **writing** that is hard to read
describe	a short dedication **written** in a book or engraved on something, such as a coin or monument
transcribe	a set of papers with **writing** that will be read and acted out
scribble	a **written** agreement to buy and read a magazine or newspaper for a set period of time
scribe	P.S.; a short bit of **writing** added after a letter is finished
inscription	to say or **write** down how something or someone looks; to use adjectives in **writing**
prescription	a piece of **writing**; a book

Greek and Latin Roots © 2004 Creative Teaching Press

Read-Around Review: scrib, script

I have the first card.
Who has the roots that mean **writing?**

I have the roots **scrib** and **script.**
Who has the word that describes a type of **writing** that young children use when first learning how to describe what is on their mind?

I have the word **scribble.**
Who has the word that names the **written** agreement you make when you agree to pay for a magazine to be mailed to you for a year or two?

I have the word **subscription.**
Who has the word that means a piece of **writing** or a book, often the first draft?

I have the word **manuscript.**
Who has the word that names what you need to do when **writing** stories so that the reader can picture what you are trying to say more clearly?

I have the word **describe.**
Who has the word that names one of the most important jobs back when **writing** was first invented?

I have the word **scribe.**
Who has the word that is usually at the end of a letter to mention one more short thought?

I have the word **postscript.**
Who has the word that names the set of papers or **writing** that actors memorize for a show or performance?

I have the word **script.**
Who has the word that names the piece of paper that must be signed by a doctor before you can pick up your medicine at the pharmacy?

I have the word **prescription.**
Who has the word that names a short dedication **written** in a book?

I have the word **inscription.**
Who has the word that tells what someone who is bilingual can do as a job or for fun?

I have the word **transcribe.**
Who has the first card?

Greek and Latin Roots © 2004 Creative Teaching Press

Name _____   Date _____

Vocabulary Quiz: scrib, script

Shade in the bubble for the correct word.

Ⓐ Ⓑ Ⓒ Ⓓ   **1.** If your teacher says that you used terrific adjectives to help readers picture the characters, then what did you do well?
     A) scribble   **B)** prescription   **C)** transcribe   **D)** describe

Ⓐ Ⓑ Ⓒ Ⓓ   **2.** We would not have books from the 1800s if it were not for the people who had this job.
     A) script   **B)** scribe   **C)** postscript   **D)** inscriptions

Ⓐ Ⓑ Ⓒ Ⓓ   **3.** Elizabeth is only a year old, so naturally when she picked up her first crayon to write it looked like this.
     A) inscription   **B)** transcribing   **C)** scribble   **D)** prescriptions

Ⓐ Ⓑ Ⓒ Ⓓ   **4.** If you pay for a year of Crafty Kids Magazine, then you get one of these.
     A) prescription   **B)** transcription   **C)** subscription   **D)** script

Ⓐ Ⓑ Ⓒ Ⓓ   **5.** For the class play, every student tried to memorize his or her lines as written on this.
     A) inscription   **B)** script   **C)** subscription   **D)** postscipt

Ⓐ Ⓑ Ⓒ Ⓓ   **6.** J. K. Rowling's original one of these brought in a million dollars at the auction! It was purchased by another famous author.
     A) postscript   **B)** inscription   **C)** prescription   **D)** manuscript

Ⓐ Ⓑ Ⓒ Ⓓ   **7.** "Dr. Vu has this ready for you," said the front office clerk.
     A) prescription   **B)** subscription   **C)** postscript   **D)** manuscript

Ⓐ Ⓑ Ⓒ Ⓓ   **8.** People who do this to books so that the blind can read them in Braille feel very good about their jobs.
     A) transcribe   **B)** prescribe   **C)** inscribe   **D)** postscript

Ⓐ Ⓑ Ⓒ Ⓓ   **9.** The tombstone in the ancient cemetery had one of these that said, "A blessing to all who met her!"
     A) transcribe   **B)** prescription   **C)** subscription   **D)** inscription

Ⓐ Ⓑ Ⓒ Ⓓ   **10.** At the end of the letter, there was one of these that said, "P.S. Don't forget the punch!"
     A) inscription   **B)** postscript   **C)** prescription   **D)** subscription

Write the correct word on the line so the sentence makes sense.

11. Ling was having a hard time _____ the Spanish book into Chinese.

12. The pharmacist will expect to see a _____ before you will get your medicine.

13. The _____ only cost $9.99 for ten issues throughout the year.

14. Where is my _____? I can't practice for the play without it!

15. Mr. Arias said, "I like all of the details you used to _____ the setting of your story. I can picture in my head exactly where the story takes place!"

Greek and Latin Roots © 2004 Creative Teaching Press

Review Test: graph and scrib, script

Shade in the bubble for the correct word.

Ⓐ Ⓑ Ⓒ Ⓓ **1.** I'm reading a book written by a person who built 100 homes for people who couldn't afford to do it themselves. He wrote the book himself. What type of book is it?
 A) biography **B)** autobiography **C)** autograph **D)** postscript

Ⓐ Ⓑ Ⓒ Ⓓ **2.** What is the name of a person who writes things down with the goal of recording information?
 A) dictator **B)** scribe **C)** seismograph **D)** inscription

Ⓐ Ⓑ Ⓒ Ⓓ **3.** What do you need to get from a doctor before you can get medicine?
 A) subscription **B)** phonograph **C)** postscript **D)** prescription

Ⓐ Ⓑ Ⓒ Ⓓ **4.** What do we call two words that are spelled the same but have different meanings?
 A) phonographs **B)** cartographs **C)** postscripts **D)** homographs

Ⓐ Ⓑ Ⓒ Ⓓ **5.** What is the area of study in which people make maps?
 A) cartography **B)** manuscripts **C)** photography **D)** biography

Ⓐ Ⓑ Ⓒ Ⓓ **6.** What do the earthquake scientists observe and study?
 A) seismographs **B)** scribbles **C)** phonographs **D)** paragraphs

Ⓐ Ⓑ Ⓒ Ⓓ **7.** What is also known as a record player since it changes the writing on a vinyl disc into sounds you can hear?
 A) homograph **B)** paragraph **C)** biography **D)** phonograph

Ⓐ Ⓑ Ⓒ Ⓓ **8.** Good writers try to do this with clear details.
 A) describe **B)** inscribe **C)** postscript **D)** manuscript

Ⓐ Ⓑ Ⓒ Ⓓ **9.** What is just like a hamburger with a top, an inside, and a bottom? It includes topic and concluding sentences and is filled with details and information.
 A) paragraph **B)** phonograph **C)** autograph **D)** subscription

Ⓐ Ⓑ Ⓒ Ⓓ **10.** What do the roots **scrib** and **script** mean?
 A) under **B)** to write **C)** to cut **D)** color

Ⓐ Ⓑ Ⓒ Ⓓ **11.** What does the root **graph** mean?
 A) under **B)** writing **C)** to cut **D)** color

Ⓐ Ⓑ Ⓒ Ⓓ ***12.** What does **bio** mean in the word *biography*?
 A) life **B)** writing **C)** self **D)** around

Ⓐ Ⓑ Ⓒ Ⓓ ***13.** What does **post** mean in the word *postscript*?
 A) again **B)** after **C)** before **D)** outside

Ⓐ Ⓑ Ⓒ Ⓓ ***14.** What does **trans** most likely mean in the word *transcribe*?
 A) across **B)** around **C)** path **D)** writing

Ⓐ Ⓑ Ⓒ Ⓓ ***15.** What does **biblio** most likely mean in the word *bibliography*?
 A) book **B)** life **C)** self **D)** writing

Greek and Latin Roots © 2004 Creative Teaching Press

Word List: cred = believe

Vocabulary	Definitions
accreditation (n)	granting approval or **belief** in a school
credential (n)	a document that proves a person is **believable**
credible (adj)	**believable;** reliable
credit (v)	to **believe** that someone will do something
creditor (n)	a person who **believes** that he will be paid back the money that he loaned
credulous (adj)	tending to **believe** too easily; easily convinced; easily fooled
creed (n)	a set of religious **beliefs** or principles
discredit (v)	to refuse to **believe;** to reject as untrue
incredible (adj)	not **believable;** improbable; unlikely
incredulous (adj)	doubting; unwilling or unable to **believe**

Greek and Latin Roots © 2004 Creative Teaching Press

Vocabulary Sort: cred

credible	tending to **believe** too easily; easily convinced; easily fooled
incredible	**believable;** reliable
creditor	not **believable;** improbable; unlikely
incredulous	to refuse to **believe;** to reject as untrue
accreditation	a document that proves a person is **believable**
credulous	a set of religious **beliefs** or principles
creed	a person who **believes** that he will be paid back the money that he loaned
credential	granting approval or **belief** in a school
credit	to **believe** that someone will do something
discredit	doubting; unwilling or unable to **believe**

Greek and Latin Roots © 2004 Creative Teaching Press

Read-Around Review: cred

I have the first card.
Who has the root that means **believe?**

I have the root **cred.**
Who has the word that describes something that is so unlikely that you can't **believe** that it actually happened?

I have the word **incredible.**
Who has the word the names a document that some people, including teachers, earn to show they are qualified for their job?

I have the word **credential.**
Who has the word that describes a person who is owed money and **believes** that the people who borrowed his or her money will pay it back?

I have the word **creditor.**
Who has the word that names what some people, groups, schools, and companies receive that makes them worthy of being **believed?**

I have the word **accreditation.**
Who has the word that describes what you do when you don't **believe** what you are hearing?

I have the word **discredit.**
Who has the word that names the set of religious **beliefs** followed by a church?

I have the word **creed.**
Who has the word that describes a person who is easily fooled and **believes** anything he or she hears?

I have the word **credulous.**
Who has the word that describes a person who is honest, reliable, and **believable** in what she says?

I have the word **credible.**
Who has the word that describes what you give to people whom you trust?

I have the word **credit.**
Who has the word that describes a person who doubts everything that he hears and has a hard time **believing** what people tell him?

I have the word **incredulous.**
Who has the first card?

Greek and Latin Roots © 2004 Creative Teaching Press

Name _____   Date _____

Vocabulary Quiz: cred

Shade in the bubble for the correct word.

Ⓐ Ⓑ Ⓒ Ⓓ   **1.** If a person has a reputation for not telling the truth, people will tend to do this to what he says.
A) discredit   **B)** incredible   **C)** credit   **D)** credential

Ⓐ Ⓑ Ⓒ Ⓓ   **2.** This person is waiting to be paid back the money that he loaned. He believes that he will get it back.
A) credential   **B)** incredible   **C)** creed   **D)** creditor

Ⓐ Ⓑ Ⓒ Ⓓ   **3.** This is a document that people, such as teachers, earn to show that they know what they are doing.
A) credential   **B)** creditor   **C)** credit   **D)** creed

Ⓐ Ⓑ Ⓒ Ⓓ   **4.** This is a word that describes a person who believes everything he hears.
A) accreditation   **B)** credential   **C)** creditor   **D)** credulous

Ⓐ Ⓑ Ⓒ Ⓓ   **5.** What do you give to someone if she follows through on what she says she will do?
A) credit   **B)** creditor   **C)** creeds   **D)** credential

Ⓐ Ⓑ Ⓒ Ⓓ   **6.** A person in jail or a friend who is always in trouble would never be described as this.
A) incredulous   **B)** credible   **C)** creditor   **D)** creed

Ⓐ Ⓑ Ⓒ Ⓓ   **7.** Schools must prove that they have high standards in order to keep this.
A) accreditation   **B)** creeds   **C)** incredulous   **D)** creditors

Ⓐ Ⓑ Ⓒ Ⓓ   **8.** Which word describes something that you have a hard time believing but really did happen?
A) incredible   **B)** credulous   **C)** creed   **D)** creditor

Ⓐ Ⓑ Ⓒ Ⓓ   **9.** A person who never believes anything she hears would be described as which of the following?
A) credible   **B)** incredulous   **C)** creditor   **D)** creed

Ⓐ Ⓑ Ⓒ Ⓓ   **10.** Each church or religious group follows one of these that may be more or less specific to its members.
A) creed   **B)** creditors   **C)** credentials   **D)** accreditation

Write the correct word on the line so the sentence makes sense.

11. After listening to her son tell a lie every day for a week, Mrs. Jamison was _____ about his story of the lost homework folder.

12. According to that church's _____, girls could only wear dresses and boys had to wear suits.

13. You deserve _____ for admitting what you did wrong before getting caught.

14. Teachers in public education have earned _____ that prove they know how to teach.

15. It was absolutely _____ that she won the lottery!

Greek and Latin Roots © 2004 Creative Teaching Press

Word List: jur, jus, jud = law; justice

Vocabulary	Definitions
abjure (v)	to give up rights; to recant
judge (n)	a person chosen to interpret **laws,** decide on a winner, or settle a controversy
jurisdiction (n)	the territory or land in which **justice** and **laws** are administered and followed
jurist (n)	an expert in **law**
jury (n)	a group of people sworn to abide by the **laws** to determine the truth
just (adj)	**lawful;** fair
justice (n)	fairness; rightfulness
justification (n)	the fact that is said to prove that something is true
justify (v)	to prove; to offer
perjury (v)	to break the **law** by lying; to break a formal promise; to break an oath

Greek and Latin Roots © 2004 Creative Teaching Press

Vocabulary Sort: jur, jus, jud

justify	a group of people sworn to abide by the **laws** to determine the truth
justice	the fact that is said to prove that something is true
judge	the territory or land in which **justice** and **laws** are administered and followed
perjury	to prove; to offer
jurist	**lawful;** fair
justification	to give up rights; to recant
abjure	to break the **law** by lying; to break a formal promise; to break an oath
just	a person chosen to interpret **laws,** decide on a winner, or settle a controversy
jury	an expert in **law**
jurisdiction	fairness; rightfulness

Greek and Latin Roots © 2004 Creative Teaching Press

Read-Around Review: jur, jus, jud

I have the first card.
Who has the roots that mean **law** or **justice?**

I have the roots **jur, jus,** and **jud.**
Who has the word that names the illegal action you commit when you lie under oath?

I have the word **perjury.**
Who has the word that names the person who settles a controversy or decides on a winner?

I have the word **judge.**
Who has the word that describes the region or area of land that is controlled by specific rules and **laws** that must be followed in that area?

I have the word **jurisdiction.**
Who has the word that names an expert in **law?**

I have the word **jurist.**
Who has the word that names the group of people who listen to both sides of a legal battle and decide on whether someone is guilty or innocent?

I have the word **jury.**
Who has the word that describes what you do when you offer excuses or reasons for your behavior?

I have the word **justify.**
Who has the word that means fairness or rightfulness?

I have the word **justice.**
Who has the word that describes what someone does when he gives up his legal rights?

I have the word **abjure.**
Who has the word that describes what a decision is if it truly is fair?

I have the word **just.**
Who has the word that names a fact that is offered to prove that what someone says is indeed the truth?

I have the word **justification.**
Who has the first card?

Greek and Latin Roots © 2004 Creative Teaching Press

Name _____   Date _____

Vocabulary Quiz: jur, jus, jud

Shade in the bubble for the correct word.

Ⓐ Ⓑ Ⓒ Ⓓ   **1.** What do you call an area of land that is governed by a person who can hold those people accountable for following specific laws?
A) jurisdiction   **B)** justification   **C)** jurist   **D)** justice

Ⓐ Ⓑ Ⓒ Ⓓ   **2.** What does every citizen have a right to in the United States?
A) judge   **B)** justice   **C)** justification   **D)** perjury

Ⓐ Ⓑ Ⓒ Ⓓ   **3.** Who is the person who leads the case in a courtroom and makes sure the lawyers conduct a fair trial?
A) jurist   **B)** perjury   **C)** jury   **D)** judge

Ⓐ Ⓑ Ⓒ Ⓓ   **4.** Who is known as an expert in law?
A) jurist   **B)** jury   **C)** jurisdiction   **D)** perjury

Ⓐ Ⓑ Ⓒ Ⓓ   **5.** When answering any test question that asks *why,* it is important to know that you are expected to do this to your answer.
A) perjury   **B)** jurisdiction   **C)** abjure   **D)** justify

Ⓐ Ⓑ Ⓒ Ⓓ   **6.** If you lie when you promise to tell the truth in a courtroom, you can be sent to jail because what is against the law?
A) justification   **B)** abjuring   **C)** perjury   **D)** jurists

Ⓐ Ⓑ Ⓒ Ⓓ   **7.** Your reasons for why it was okay to be home fifteen minutes late are known as these.
A) justifications   **B)** jurisdictions   **C)** perjury   **D)** justice

Ⓐ Ⓑ Ⓒ Ⓓ   **8.** As a citizen you may do this.
A) abjure   **B)** perjury   **C)** jurisdiction   **D)** justice

Ⓐ Ⓑ Ⓒ Ⓓ   **9.** A decision that is fair is also what?
A) just   **B)** abjured   **C)** jurisdiction   **D)** jurist

Ⓐ Ⓑ Ⓒ Ⓓ   **10.** A fair trial for any suspect requires which of the following?
A) jury   **B)** justification   **C)** abjure   **D)** perjury

Write the correct word on the line so the sentence makes sense.

11. The judge said, "As the members of the _____, you must promise to listen to both sides with an open mind."

12. Wow! You're quite a _____. I didn't know you knew so much about the law!

13. You may not take _____ into your own hands.

14. The man who was running for mayor threw a huge party with food and fireworks for all of the people in his _____.

15. Take responsibility for your mistakes; don't try to _____ them.

Greek and Latin Roots © 2004 Creative Teaching Press

Name _____   Date _____

Review Test: cred and jur, jus, jud

Shade in the bubble for the correct word.

Ⓐ Ⓑ Ⓒ Ⓓ   1. When trying to tell someone the right thing to do in a situation, it's important to be which of the following?
   A) incredulous   **B)** justified   **C)** discredit   **D)** credible

Ⓐ Ⓑ Ⓒ Ⓓ   2. If someone believes that you will really do something, she will give you this.
   A) credit   **B)** accreditation   **C)** credential   **D)** justice

Ⓐ Ⓑ Ⓒ Ⓓ   3. When you try to make excuses for your actions, whether they are right or wrong, you are offering what?
   A) perjury   **B)** justifications   **C)** credentials   **D)** credit

Ⓐ Ⓑ Ⓒ Ⓓ   4. An area or region that is ruled, governed, or controlled by a certain person is said to be in that person's what?
   A) jurisdiction   **B)** justification   **C)** accreditation   **D)** justice

Ⓐ Ⓑ Ⓒ Ⓓ   5. Which of the following is against the law in a courtroom?
   A) justice   **B)** perjury   **C)** creeds   **D)** abjuring

Ⓐ Ⓑ Ⓒ Ⓓ   6. What is the name of the group of people who listen to a court case to decide whether or not a person deserves to be punished?
   A) jury   **B)** judge   **C)** creditor   **D)** jurist

Ⓐ Ⓑ Ⓒ Ⓓ   7. What is the name of the document people go to school for to prove that they are educated enough to do a certain job?
   A) credential   **B)** perjury   **C)** credit   **D)** justice

Ⓐ Ⓑ Ⓒ Ⓓ   8. What do police officers try to uphold?
   A) justice   **B)** perjury   **C)** jurists   **D)** accreditation

Ⓐ Ⓑ Ⓒ Ⓓ   9. This word describes a person who never believes what people say just because they say it.
   A) credulous   **B)** just   **C)** justified   **D)** incredulous

Ⓐ Ⓑ Ⓒ Ⓓ   10. What do the roots **jur, jus,** and **jud** mean?
   A) rule   **B)** law   **C)** to cut   **D)** to write

Ⓐ Ⓑ Ⓒ Ⓓ   11. What does the root **cred** mean?
   A) believe   **B)** law   **C)** to cut   **D)** to write

Ⓐ Ⓑ Ⓒ Ⓓ   *12. What does **dis** mean in the word *discredit*?
   A) not   **B)** half   **C)** over   **D)** believe

Ⓐ Ⓑ Ⓒ Ⓓ   *13. What does **in** mean in the words *incredulous* and *incredible*?
   A) not   **B)** within   **C)** after   **D)** outside

Ⓐ Ⓑ Ⓒ Ⓓ   14. If you owe someone money, who do you need to pay back?
   A) jurist   **B)** judge   **C)** accreditation   **D)** creditor

Ⓐ Ⓑ Ⓒ Ⓓ   15. Who settles a disagreement in a courtroom, a swimming pool, or a pie eating contest?
   A) jurist   **B)** creditor   **C)** jury   **D)** judge

Greek and Latin Roots © 2004 Creative Teaching Press

Word List: ben, bene, bon = good, well

Vocabulary	Definitions
benediction (n)	a **good** blessing in a religious service
benefactor (n)	a **good** person who offers help or donates money
beneficial (adj)	having a **good** outcome; favorable
beneficiary (n)	a person who receives something **good** from someone else such as an inheritance
benefit (v)	to gain or receive **good** results from something
benevolent (adj)	kind; **good**-hearted
benign (adj)	favorable; having a **good** effect; not harmful
bonafide (adj)	in **good** faith; authentic; genuine; real
bonus (n)	anything **good** that is received over and beyond what was expected (usually money)
bon voyage (n)	French for "have a **good** trip"

Vocabulary Sort: ben, bene, bon

beneficial	kind; **good**-hearted
bonafide	having a **good** outcome; favorable
benefactor	favorable; having a **good** effect; not harmful
benefit	a **good** blessing in a religious service
benign	anything **good** that is received over and beyond what was expected (usually money)
bon voyage	French for "have a **good** trip"
benediction	in **good** faith; authentic; genuine; real
bonus	a person who receives something **good** from someone else such as an inheritance
beneficiary	to gain or receive **good** results from something
benevolent	a **good** person who offers help or donates money

Greek and Latin Roots © 2004 Creative Teaching Press

Read-Around Review: ben, bene, bon

I have the first card.
Who has the roots that mean **good?**

I have the roots **ben, bene** and **bon.**
Who has the word that identifies the person who gets something **good** such as an inheritance?

I have the word **beneficiary.**
Who has the word that describes a **good**-hearted, kind person or character?

I have the word **benevolent.**
Who has the word that describes something that is real and authentic?

I have the word **bonafide.**
Who has the word that names anything that is over and beyond what is expected that is given to a person?

I have the word **bonus.**
Who has the word that describes something that is **good** and will have a **good** outcome?

I have the word **beneficial.**
Who has the word that identifies a person who helps others in need, often by donating money?

I have the word **benefactor.**
Who has the word that describes something that has a **good** or favorable effect?

I have the word **benign.**
Who has the phrase that people say when they are wishing friends or family to have a **good** trip?

I have the word **bon voyage.**
Who has the word that names the **good** blessing that is said in some religious services?

I have the word **benediction.**
Who has the word that describes what you will do if you get something that produces **good** results for you?

I have the word **benefit.**
Who has the first card?

Greek and Latin Roots © 2004 Creative Teaching Press

Name _____   Date _____

Vocabulary Quiz: ben, bene, bon

Shade in the bubble for the correct word.

Ⓐ Ⓑ Ⓒ Ⓓ   **1.** Which word is sometimes used to describe a document or on ancient artifact that is genuine?
   A) bonus   **B)** benefit   **C)** beneficiary   **D)** bonafide

Ⓐ Ⓑ Ⓒ Ⓓ   **2.** At holiday time, many companies give this to each employee in the form of extra money.
   A) benefit   **B)** bonus   **C)** benediction   **D)** bon voyage

Ⓐ Ⓑ Ⓒ Ⓓ   **3.** The university was grateful to this person who donated five educational scholarships worth $10,000. Who was the person?
   A) benefactor   **B)** beneficiary   **C)** benevolent   **D)** benediction

Ⓐ Ⓑ Ⓒ Ⓓ   **4.** A kind person who helps others might be described as this.
   A) benign   **B)** beneficiaries   **C)** bonafides   **D)** benevolent

Ⓐ Ⓑ Ⓒ Ⓓ   **5.** This is what you will do if you study hard and try your best.
   A) benefit   **B)** beneficiary   **C)** benign   **D)** bonus

Ⓐ Ⓑ Ⓒ Ⓓ   **6.** Vitamins are _____ to good health and a long life.
   A) beneficial   **B)** benign   **C)** bon voyage   **D)** benediction

Ⓐ Ⓑ Ⓒ Ⓓ   **7.** Who gets things that are left behind when a person passes away?
   A) beneficiary   **B)** benefactor   **C)** benediction   **D)** bonafide

Ⓐ Ⓑ Ⓒ Ⓓ   **8.** What did Grandma Dot yell to her family when they left on the cruise?
   A) bonafide   **B)** benign   **C)** benevolent   **D)** bon voyage

Ⓐ Ⓑ Ⓒ Ⓓ   **9.** Sometimes people get tumors that are not harmful. What do we call this type of tumor?
   A) benign   **B)** bonafide   **C)** bonuses   **D)** benediction

Ⓐ Ⓑ Ⓒ Ⓓ   **10.** The members of the church listened closely to this.
   A) benediction   **B)** beneficial   **C)** bonafide   **D)** beneficiary

Write the correct word on the line so the sentence makes sense.

11. "Look! I received _____ points on my report for having it neatly organized!"

12. It's _____ to your future success to try your best throughout your school years.

13. The main character was _____ when she gave her last bit of water to the thirsty child.

14. The generous _____ gave the museum three expensive original paintings for the public to enjoy viewing.

15. "That coin is a _____ Susan B. Anthony silver dollar!"

Greek and Latin Roots © 2004 Creative Teaching Press

Word List: mal, male = bad; abnormal; worse

Vocabulary	Definitions
dismal (adj)	depressing; causing gloom or misery; causing **bad** feelings
malady (n)	**bad** health; illness; sickness
malaria (n)	**bad** air; a disease usually spread by infected mosquitoes
malefactor (n)	an evildoer; a person who does **bad** things
malevolent (adj)	a word that describes a person or character who wishes **bad** things would happen to others
malfeasance (n)	wrongdoing or **bad** conduct by a public official
malice (n)	mischief; evil intent; **bad** will
malignant (adj)	harmful; something **bad** enough that it could result in death when related to cancer
malnourished (adj)	having **bad** health or having poor nutrition
malodorous (adj)	**bad** smell; stinky

Greek and Latin Roots © 2004 Creative Teaching Press

Vocabulary Sort: mal, male

malefactor	a word that describes a person or character who wishes **bad** things would happen to others
malice	wrongdoing or **bad** conduct by a public official
malnourished	**bad** smell; stinky
dismal	mischief; evil intent; **bad** will
malodorous	**bad** air; a disease usually spread by infected mosquitoes
malaria	having **bad** health or having poor nutrition
malignant	harmful; something **bad** enough that it could result in death when related to cancer
malfeasance	depressing; causing gloom or misery; causing **bad** feelings
malady	**bad** health; illness; sickness
malevolent	an evildoer; a person who does **bad** things

Greek and Latin Roots © 2004 Creative Teaching Press

Read-Around Review: mal, male

I have the first card.
Who has the roots that mean **bad?**

I have the roots **mal** and **male.**
Who has the word that names what a public official would be charged with if he did something wrong while in office or showed **bad** conduct?

I have the word **malfeasance.**
Who has the word that describes a person who is very unhealthy and has poor eating habits?

I have the word **malnourished.**
Who has the word that identifies a character in a story who does **bad** things?

I have the word **malefactor.**
Who has the word that names the deadly disease that is spread through **bad** air by infected mosquitoes?

I have the word **malaria.**
Who has the word that describes a terrible rotten egg smell?

I have the word **malodorous.**
Who has the word that names an illness or sickness that a person may be suffering from?

I have the word **malady.**
Who has the word that describes **bad** will or mischief shown by a person?

I have the word **malice.**
Who has the word that is usually related to something harmful such as a cancerous tumor?

I have the word **malignant.**
Who has the word that describes the behavior of a **bad** character or villain in a story?

I have the word **malevolent.**
Who has the word that describes a very sad event or situation in which everyone just feels gloomy and down?

I have the word **dismal.**
Who has the first card?

Greek and Latin Roots © 2004 Creative Teaching Press

Vocabulary Quiz: mal, male

Shade in the bubble for the correct word.

Ⓐ Ⓑ Ⓒ Ⓓ   **1.** Most stories have good and bad characters. Which word would most likely describe the bad characters in most books?
   A) malnourished   **B)** malodorous   **C)** malignant   **D)** malevolent

Ⓐ Ⓑ Ⓒ Ⓓ   **2.** If a public official was caught doing something illegal or against good judgement, what might he be punished for?
   A) malfeasance   **B)** malefactor   **C)** malady   **D)** malaria

Ⓐ Ⓑ Ⓒ Ⓓ   **3.** Sometimes people become this because they cannot afford to buy healthy foods, clean water, or vitamins.
   A) malodorous   **B)** malnourished   **C)** malady   **D)** malignant

Ⓐ Ⓑ Ⓒ Ⓓ   **4.** Dr. Cell specializes in cancer research to help people who have tumors that are described as which of the following?
   A) malignant   **B)** malice   **C)** malodorous   **D)** malaria

Ⓐ Ⓑ Ⓒ Ⓓ   **5.** Luckily, this disease is rarely found in the United States.
   A) malefactor   **B)** malice   **C)** malaria   **D)** malignant

Ⓐ Ⓑ Ⓒ Ⓓ   **6.** Most people go to the doctor and describe their symptoms so the doctor can identify this.
   A) malady   **B)** malnourished   **C)** malice   **D)** malefactors

Ⓐ Ⓑ Ⓒ Ⓓ   **7.** You can usually describe a trash can or trash dumpster with this word.
   A) malnourished   **B)** malaria   **C)** malodorous   **D)** dismal

Ⓐ Ⓑ Ⓒ Ⓓ   **8.** This person is the villain who does the mean things in the story.
   A) malefactor   **B)** malice   **C)** malignant   **D)** malady

Ⓐ Ⓑ Ⓒ Ⓓ   **9.** This word is usually related to bad behavior or wishing something bad would happen to someone.
   A) malady   **B)** malefactor   **C)** dismal   **D)** malice

Ⓐ Ⓑ Ⓒ Ⓓ   **10.** If you are feeling down, sad, or just unhappy over a scene in a story or a situation that happened to you in real life, then you might feel that things are a bit like this.
   A) dismal   **B)** malignant   **C)** malevolent   **D)** malnourished

Write the correct word on the line so the sentence makes sense.

11. Scott was feeling _____ after he found out that the movie he was waiting for three weeks to see on opening day was sold out.

12. If you don't know what your _____ is, then you might want to visit a doctor.

13. The mayor of the city was punished for _____ due to his mismanagement of the city's money.

14. To prevent becoming _____, it is wise to eat healthy foods and take a daily vitamin.

15. The _____ was punished at the end of the story. He deserved it!

Greek and Latin Roots © 2004 Creative Teaching Press

Name _____   Date _____

Review Test: ben, bene, bon and mal, male

Shade in the bubble for the correct word.

Ⓐ Ⓑ Ⓒ Ⓓ   **1.** What word might you hear a person leading an auction say when trying to get people to bid on an ancient piece of pottery?
A) benign   **B)** bonafide   **C)** malice   **D)** dismal

Ⓐ Ⓑ Ⓒ Ⓓ   **2.** What might a governor be accused of if he makes a very bad choice while in office?
A) malfeasance   **B)** benefits   **C)** bon voyage   **D)** malady

Ⓐ Ⓑ Ⓒ Ⓓ   **3.** What do you call someone who donates money to charity or gives expensive items to be sold for money?
A) malefactor   **B)** beneficiary   **C)** malevolent   **D)** benefactor

Ⓐ Ⓑ Ⓒ Ⓓ   **4.** Which word describes a sad feeling?
A) malevolent   **B)** bonus   **C)** dismal   **D)** beneficial

Ⓐ Ⓑ Ⓒ Ⓓ   **5.** What do you often hear people say to friends who are leaving on a cruise?
A) bonus   **B)** bon voyage   **C)** malaria   **D)** benefit

Ⓐ Ⓑ Ⓒ Ⓓ   **6.** Which word describes someone who wants bad things to happen to other people?
A) benevolent   **B)** malignant   **C)** malevolent   **D)** dismal

Ⓐ Ⓑ Ⓒ Ⓓ   **7.** What do adults love getting from their boss around the holidays?
A) bonus   **B)** malaria   **C)** benefactors   **D)** malice

Ⓐ Ⓑ Ⓒ Ⓓ   **8.** What do we call an act that shows an evil intent?
A) benevolent   **B)** malice   **C)** malnourished   **D)** beneficial

Ⓐ Ⓑ Ⓒ Ⓓ   **9.** If you walk into an alley on trash pick-up day, which word would best describe it?
A) benign   **B)** malignant   **C)** malice   **D)** malodorous

Ⓐ Ⓑ Ⓒ Ⓓ   **10.** What do the roots **mal** and **male** mean?
A) bad   **B)** good   **C)** to break   **D)** together

Ⓐ Ⓑ Ⓒ Ⓓ   **11.** What do the roots **ben, bene,** and **bon** mean?
A) bad   **B)** good   **C)** to break   **D)** together

Ⓐ Ⓑ Ⓒ Ⓓ   ***12.** What does the suffix- **or** mean in the words *benefactor* and *malefactor*?
A) a person who   **B)** apart   **C)** together   **D)** friendly

Ⓐ Ⓑ Ⓒ Ⓓ   **13.** Finish this analogy: good : bad :: _____ · _____ .
A) benign : malignant   **B)** malignant : benign
C) benefit : malaria   **D)** malfeasance : bonus

Ⓐ Ⓑ Ⓒ Ⓓ   **14.** Which character is often the "bad guy" or villain in a story or movie?
A) benefactor   **B)** malefactor   **C)** beneficiary   **D)** malice

Ⓐ Ⓑ Ⓒ Ⓓ   **15.** If you work hard it will be _____ to your future success.
A) beneficial   **B)** benign   **C)** malevolent   **D)** malady

Greek and Latin Roots © 2004 Creative Teaching Press

Word List: bio = life

Vocabulary	Definitions
antibiotic (n)	a medicine used to save **lives** because it destroys harmful bacteria and cures infections
autobiography (n)	a piece of writing written by a person about his or her own **life**
biography (n)	a piece of writing about a person's **life** written by someone else
biologist (n)	a person who studies **living** things
biology (n)	the study of **living** things
biopsy (n)	the removal of **living** tissue from the body for diagnostic examination
biosphere (n)	the zone of planet Earth where there is **life** (between the deep crust and the lower atmosphere)
macrobiotic diet (n)	a diet thought to help people **live** longer because it focuses on natural foods
neurobiology (n)	the study of the nervous system of **living** things and how it helps the **living** things learn and react
symbiosis (n)	how two different **living** organisms **live** together and depend on each other

Greek and Latin Roots © 2004 Creative Teaching Press

Vocabulary Sort: bio

biography	the study of **living** things
antibiotic	the zone of planet Earth where there is **life** (between the deep crust and the lower atmosphere)
biologist	a medicine used to save **lives** because it destroys harmful bacteria and cures infections
biosphere	a diet thought to help people **live** longer because it focuses on natural foods
neurobiology	the removal of **living** tissue from the body for diagnostic examination
symbiosis	a piece of writing written by a person about his or her own **life**
biology	the study of the nervous system of **living** things and how it helps the **living** things learn and react
macrobiotic diet	a piece of writing about a person's **life** written by someone else
biopsy	a person who studies **living** things
autobiography	how two different **living** organisms **live** together and depend on each other

Greek and Latin Roots © 2004 Creative Teaching Press

Read-Around Review: bio

I have the first card.
Who has the root that means **life?**

I have the root **bio.**
Who has the word that names the scientist who studies **living** things?

I have the word **biologist.**
Who has the word that names the zone of Earth where there are **living** things?

I have the word **biosphere.**
Who has the word that describes the relationship between **living** things that depend on each other and **live** together in the same environment?

I have the word **symbiosis.**
Who has the word that names the type of book that is about a person's **life** but was written by someone else?

I have the word **biography.**
Who has the word that names the diet thought to help people **live** longer because it focuses on natural foods?

I have the word **macrobiotic diet.**
Who has the word that identifies the type of book that is written about a person's **life** by that actual person?

I have the word **autobiography.**
Who has the word that labels the types of medicine that help people **live** by destroying any harmful bacteria that got into a person's body?

I have the word **antibiotics.**
Who has the word that names the medical procedure done by surgeons that removes part of **living** tissue from a person's body to investigate it for disease?

I have the word **biopsy.**
Who has the word that names the field of study that focuses on **living** things?

I have the word **biology.**
Who has the word that labels the study of the nervous systems of **living** things?

I have the word **neurobiology.**
Who has the first card?

Greek and Latin Roots © 2004 Creative Teaching Press

Vocabulary Quiz: bio

Shade in the bubble for the correct word.

Ⓐ Ⓑ Ⓒ Ⓓ   **1.** If you want to study living things when you go to college, what might you want to become in your future?
A) biologist   **B)** biography   **C)** antibiotic   **D)** neurobiologist

Ⓐ Ⓑ Ⓒ Ⓓ   **2.** If Michael Jordan decides to write a book about his life growing up and becoming a basketball player, what kind of book would it be?
A) biography   **B)** biology   **C)** symbiosis   **D)** autobiography

Ⓐ Ⓑ Ⓒ Ⓓ   **3.** The doctor was performing this surgery to examine the tissue for cancer cells.
A) biosphere   **B)** neurobiology   **C)** antibiotic   **D)** biopsy

Ⓐ Ⓑ Ⓒ Ⓓ   **4.** Which layer of Earth has the living things?
A) atmosphere   **B)** biosphere   **C)** core   **D)** galaxy

Ⓐ Ⓑ Ⓒ Ⓓ   **5.** Devon eats mostly natural foods because he believes they will help him live longer. What type of diet does he have?
A) neurobiology   **B)** biology   **C)** macrobiotic   **D)** antibiotics

Ⓐ Ⓑ Ⓒ Ⓓ   **6.** When studying how living things share the same living space and get along, what relationship are you looking at?
A) symbiosis   **B)** biography   **C)** biology   **D)** neurobiology

Ⓐ Ⓑ Ⓒ Ⓓ   **7.** There are many books written about the famous artist Vincent Van Gogh. They are what type of book?
A) antibiotics   **B)** biographies   **C)** biology   **D)** autobiographies

Ⓐ Ⓑ Ⓒ Ⓓ   **8.** When you have an infection, what might a doctor prescribe?
A) antibiotics   **B)** biology   **C)** biographies   **D)** a biopsy

Ⓐ Ⓑ Ⓒ Ⓓ   **9.** Which type of science investigates living things?
A) neurobiology   **B)** biography   **C)** autobiography   **D)** biology

Ⓐ Ⓑ Ⓒ Ⓓ   **10.** Which branch of science investigates how the brain affects the body?
A) neurobiology   **B)** biography   **C)** autobiography   **D)** biology

Write the correct word on the line so the sentence makes sense.

11. Have you had a chance to read the book Michael J. Fox wrote about his life? It's a terrific
_____.

12. Only a doctor can give you _____ to make you healthy again.

13. One of the most popular science classes in high school and college is _____ because you get to learn about living things.

14. The tropical rain forests are excellent locations to observe _____ in action, since there are so many different species of plants and animals living in the same space and depending on each other for survival.

15. We live in the _____ of planet Earth.

Greek and Latin Roots © 2004 Creative Teaching Press

Word List: vit, viv = live; life

Vocabulary	Definitions
revitalize (v)	to bring something back after it declined in condition or popularity; to breathe new **life** into something
revive (v)	to bring back to **life** again
survival (n)	the ability to continue **living**
survivor (n)	a person who **lives** through a difficult event or experience
vital (adj)	necessary or essential to **life**
vitality (n)	quality or state of being full of **life;** state of being full of energy
vitamin (n)	a tablet of substances that are thought to promote a healthy **life**
vivacious (adj)	full of **life;** fun; lively; animated
vivid (adj)	"as big as **life**"; brightly colored; daring
vivisection (n)	surgery on **living** animals; medical research that involves cutting into animals to study organs, parts, or diseases

Greek and Latin Roots © 2004 Creative Teaching Press

Vocabulary Sort: vit, viv

revive	"as big as **life**"; brightly colored; daring
vital	a tablet of substances that are thought to promote a healthy **life**
vivacious	surgery on **living** animals; medical research that involves cutting into animals to study organs, parts, or diseases
survivor	necessary or essential to **life**
revitalize	quality or state of being full of **life;** state of being full of energy
vivid	the ability to continue **living**
vivisection	full of **life;** fun; lively; animated
survival	a person who **lives** through a difficult event or experience
vitality	to bring something back after it declined in condition or popularity; to breathe new **life** into something
vitamin	to bring back to **life** again

Read-Around Review: vit, viv

I have the first card.
Who has the roots that mean **live** and **life?**

I have the roots **vit** and **viv.**
Who has the word that describes a **lively** person who is always fun?

I have the word **vivacious.**
Who has the word that identifies the tablet that many people take to promote a long and healthy **life?**

I have the word **vitamin.**
Who has the word that describes something that is necessary for **life?**

I have the word **vital.**
Who has the word that identifies a person who **lives** through a difficult event or experience?

I have the word **survivor.**
Who has the word that describes things such as clothing or art that are colorful?

I have the word **vivid.**
Who has the word that describes what people focus on when lost in the woods because they just want to keep on **living?**

I have the word **survival.**
Who has the word that describes what you do when you bring something back to **life?**

I have the word **revive.**
Who has the word that names the surgery some scientists perform on **living** animals to research medicines?

I have the word **vivisection.**
Who has the word that describes what a person does when he tries to bring back something that was once popular?

I have the word **revitalize.**
Who has the word that names the quality or state of being full of **life** or energy?

I have the word **vitality.**
Who has the first card?

Greek and Latin Roots © 2004 Creative Teaching Press

Name _____   Date _____

Vocabulary Quiz: vit, viv

Shade in the bubble for the correct word.

Ⓐ Ⓑ Ⓒ Ⓓ **1.** What do some cities try to do to their downtown areas to bring in more visitors and therefore more money?
    A) vivisect   **B)** vivid   **C)** survival   **D)** revitalize

Ⓐ Ⓑ Ⓒ Ⓓ **2.** People who are faced with life-threatening illnesses tend to focus on this.
    A) vivisection   **B)** survival   **C)** vitamins   **D)** reviving

Ⓐ Ⓑ Ⓒ Ⓓ **3.** There are many marathons around the world for these people who had an illness but overcame it to live long healthy lives.
    A) survivors   **B)** vivids   **C)** vivisections   **D)** revivals

Ⓐ Ⓑ Ⓒ Ⓓ **4.** If someone says that you are full of energy, you would have this.
    A) vitality   **B)** revived   **C)** survivor   **D)** vivid

Ⓐ Ⓑ Ⓒ Ⓓ **5.** A healthy heart is this in relation to your life.
    A) survival   **B)** vivisection   **C)** vivacious   **D)** vital

Ⓐ Ⓑ Ⓒ Ⓓ **6.** Health food stores sell many of these to people who want to live longer.
    A) vitamins   **B)** vivids   **C)** vivisections   **D)** survivors

Ⓐ Ⓑ Ⓒ Ⓓ **7.** Doctors are sometimes able to do this to people in the emergency room.
    A) survive   **B)** vivisection   **C)** revive   **D)** vivid

Ⓐ Ⓑ Ⓒ Ⓓ **8.** The scientist researching kidney disease used the kidney of a monkey for his research. What might he have performed?
    A) vivisection   **B)** vivacious   **C)** survival   **D)** vitamins

Ⓐ Ⓑ Ⓒ Ⓓ **9.** Erin said, "The surfboards on that shirt are as big as life!" What were they really?
    A) vivid   **B)** survival   **C)** revived   **D)** vitamins

Ⓐ Ⓑ Ⓒ Ⓓ **10.** The three-year-old girl won the spot on the commercial because she was so outgoing, friendly, and funny. What else was she?
    A) revived   **B)** survivor   **C)** vivid   **D)** vivacious

Write the correct word on the line so the sentence makes sense.

11. The speaker at the conference told the audience that she was a cancer _____.

12. The beach towel was so _____ that the man had to wear his sunglasses as he walked by.

13. The teacher was so _____ that she made every child in her class excited to go to school every day.

14. Did you take your _____ today? You know they keep you healthy!

15. The Oldies But Goodies Band was trying to _____ the popularity of old big band music from the early 1900s.

Greek and Latin Roots © 2004 Creative Teaching Press

Name _____   Date _____

Review Test: bio and vit, viv

Shade in the bubble for the correct word.

Ⓐ Ⓑ Ⓒ Ⓓ   **1.** Name the scientist who studies living things.
    A) biographer   **B)** neurobiologist   **C)** autobiographer **D)** biologist

Ⓐ Ⓑ Ⓒ Ⓓ   **2.** What are you if you were in danger of disease or illness but you came out of it healthy and even more alive?
    A) biopsy   **B)** survivor   **C)** antibiotic   **D)** vital

Ⓐ Ⓑ Ⓒ Ⓓ   **3.** Which word is the layer of Earth in which we live with all other living things?
    A) biosphere   **B)** vivisection   **C)** revival   **D)** biology

Ⓐ Ⓑ Ⓒ Ⓓ   **4.** When a doctor removes a small piece of tissue from a living person to investigate it under the microscope, what is he or she doing?
    A) vivisection   **B)** biopsy   **C)** macrobiotics   **D)** neurobiology

Ⓐ Ⓑ Ⓒ Ⓓ   **5.** What got its name because people believed that if you took it you might live a longer and healthier life?
    A) vitamin   **B)** vivisection   **C)** biosphere   **D)** biopsy

Ⓐ Ⓑ Ⓒ Ⓓ   **6.** What kind of book are you reading if it's about a Roman emperor and was written by a historical researcher named Keith Noslo?
    A) autobiography **B)** biology   **C)** biography   **D)** biopsy

Ⓐ Ⓑ Ⓒ Ⓓ   **7.** If you are trying to bring your plant back to life by moving it into the sunshine, what are you hoping to do to it?
    A) vivisection   **B)** biopsy   **C)** revive   **D)** survive

Ⓐ Ⓑ Ⓒ Ⓓ   **8.** The food chain in any environment explains how this works.
    A) symbiosis   **B)** biology   **C)** neurobiology   **D)** macrobiotics

Ⓐ Ⓑ Ⓒ Ⓓ   **9.** A person who makes everyone smile and laugh at a party might be described using this word.
    A) vivacious   **B)** vital   **C)** biologist   **D)** survivor

Ⓐ Ⓑ Ⓒ Ⓓ   **10.** What does the root **viv** mean?
    A) life, live   **B)** to throw or toss   **C)** to speak   **D)** health

Ⓐ Ⓑ Ⓒ Ⓓ   **11.** What does the root **bio** mean?
    A) life   **B)** to throw or toss   **C)** to speak   **D)** health

Ⓐ Ⓑ Ⓒ Ⓓ   ***12.** What does **sym** mean in the word *symbiosis*?
    A) apart   **B)** together   **C)** forest   **D)** across

Ⓐ Ⓑ Ⓒ Ⓓ   ***13.** What does **re** mean in the words *revive* and *revitalize*?
    A) again   **B)** within   **C)** after   **D)** outside

Ⓐ Ⓑ Ⓒ Ⓓ   **14.** What does **bio** most likely mean in the words *biography* and *biology*?
    A) life   **B)** writing   **C)** path   **D)** helping

Ⓐ Ⓑ Ⓒ Ⓓ   **15.** Which word reflects what your heart and lungs are for your survival?
    A) viable   **B)** vital   **C)** bioptic   **D)** vivid

Greek and Latin Roots © 2004 Creative Teaching Press

Word List: flect, flex = bend

Vocabulary	Definitions
circumflex (n)	to **bend** around or curve
deflect (v)	to turn or move to one side; to **bend;** to swerve
flexible (adj)	capable of **bending** without breaking
flexor (n)	a muscle that **bends** a part of the body, such as an arm or a leg
inflection (n)	the **bending** of a person's voice so that it does not sound boring or within only one tone; making one's voice go up and down
inflexible (adj)	not capable of being **bent** without breaking
reflect (v)	to **bend** or throw back light or heat; to fold or turn back
reflection (n)	the image in a mirror that is a result of **bending** light when it is thrown back
reflex angle (n)	an angle that is greater than 180 degrees because the angle is **bent** beyond the straight line
retroflex (adj)	**bent** or turned backward

Greek and Latin Roots © 2004 Creative Teaching Press

Vocabulary Sort: flect, flex

deflect	capable of **bending** without breaking
retroflex	to **bend** or throw back light or heat; to fold or turn back
reflection	an angle that is greater than 180 degrees because the angle is **bent** beyond the straight line
inflection	the image in a mirror that is a result of **bending** light when it is thrown back
flexor	the **bending** of a person's voice so that it does not sound boring or within only one tone; making one's voice go up and down
reflect	to **bend** around or curve
reflex angle	to turn or move to one side; to **bend;** to swerve
inflexible	**bent** or turned backward
circumflex	a muscle that **bends** a part of the body, such as an arm or a leg
flexible	capable of **bending** without breaking

Greek and Latin Roots © 2004 Creative Teaching Press

Read-Around Review: flect, flex

I have the first card.
Who has the roots that mean **bend?**

I have the roots **flect** and **flex.**
Who has the word that describes what you are if you can't **bend** a certain way?

I have the word **inflexible.**
Who has the word that describes what happens to light when it is **bent** and seems to be thrown back at you?

I have the word **reflect.**
Who has the word that names the type of angle that **bends** back beyond the 180 degrees of a straight line?

I have the word **reflex angle.**
Who has the word that names the type of muscle that **bends** a part of the body, such as an arm or a leg?

I have the word **flexor.**
Who has the word that names what you see in a mirror as a result of **bent** light?

I have the word **reflection.**
Who has the word that describes someone who can **bend** all the way down to touch her toes or do the splits?

I have the word **flexible.**
Who has the word that labels what you do with your voice when you are a good reader and it goes up and down to show excitement or sadness within a story?

I have the word **inflection.**
Who has the word that names what you do when you try to keep something away from you so you **bend** or swerve in the other direction?

I have the word **deflect.**
Who has the word that describes what something can do if it can **bend** around or curve?

I have the word **circumflex.**
Who has the word that describes what something is when it is **bent** or turned backward?

I have the word **retroflex.**
Who has the first card?

Greek and Latin Roots © 2004 Creative Teaching Press

Vocabulary Quiz: flect, flex

Shade in the bubble for the correct word.

Ⓐ Ⓑ Ⓒ Ⓓ **1.** A bulletproof vest is designed to do this to a bullet to protect police officers and military personnel.
A) flexor **B)** reflect **C)** deflect **D)** inflexible

Ⓐ Ⓑ Ⓒ Ⓓ **2.** It is important for ballet dancers to be this.
A) inflexible **B)** flexible **C)** circumflex **D)** reflections

Ⓐ Ⓑ Ⓒ Ⓓ **3.** Your arms and legs have these muscles to allow bending movements.
A) flexor **B)** circumflex **C)** retroflex **D)** reflective

Ⓐ Ⓑ Ⓒ Ⓓ **4.** Name the angle that bends all the way back beyond the angle of a straight line.
A) circumflex **B)** reflex **C)** inflective **D)** retroflex

Ⓐ Ⓑ Ⓒ Ⓓ **5.** Something that is bent or turned backward is in what physical state?
A) retroflex **B)** inflexibility **C)** reflections **D)** deflect

Ⓐ Ⓑ Ⓒ Ⓓ **6.** Books on tape always use readers who show this in their voices.
A) reflexing **B)** inflexibility **C)** reflexes **D)** inflection

Ⓐ Ⓑ Ⓒ Ⓓ **7.** When making a solar cooker, it is important to figure out how to do this to the sun to melt the cheese on your nachos.
A) reflect **B)** deflect **C)** circumblex **D)** flexible

Ⓐ Ⓑ Ⓒ Ⓓ **8.** Your wrist is able to do this pretty well.
A) circumflex **B)** inflex **C)** reflex **D)** deflect

Ⓐ Ⓑ Ⓒ Ⓓ **9.** People who have a hard time in yoga classes can be described as this.
A) inflexible **B)** flexible **C)** circumflex **D)** deflect

Ⓐ Ⓑ Ⓒ Ⓓ **10.** Did you see how that mirror bent the light to show the image clearly? What was seen?
A) inflexibility **B)** flexor **C)** reflex **D)** reflection

Write the correct word on the line so the sentence makes sense.

11. Some people have many mirrors around the house because they love to admire their

_____.

12. Stretching every day will help a person who is _____ become more

_____.

13. The racket _____ the ball in the wrong direction, so the tennis star lost the match.

14. The ballerina was so _____ that she could lift her leg up to touch her nose.

15. When light is bent back, it is _____.

Greek and Latin Roots © 2004 Creative Teaching Press

Word List: frail, fract, frag = break; shatter

Vocabulary	Definitions
fractals (n)	the type of geometry that creates **broken** patterns out of a smaller version of a design
fraction (n)	a part of a whole; a **broken** piece of something that is no longer whole
fracture (n)	a **break** in a part of the body
fragile (adj)	so delicate that it could **break** easily; easily damaged
fragment (n)	an incomplete sentence; a **break** in a sentence
fragmented (adj)	describes something that is **broken** into pieces
frail (adj)	being easily **broken** or destroyed
infraction (n)	a **broken** rule; a violation
refract (v)	to bend light so that it looks like it is **broken**
suffrage (v)	to **break** into an issue; to vote

Greek and Latin Roots © 2004 Creative Teaching Press

Vocabulary Sort: frail, fract, frag

fragile	an incomplete sentence; a **break** in a sentence
fracture	the type of geometry that creates **broken** patterns out of a smaller version of a design
fragmented	a part of a whole; a **broken** piece of something that is no longer whole
infraction	to **break** into an issue; to vote
refract	so delicate that it could **break** easily; easily damaged
suffrage	a **broken** rule; a violation
fragment	to bend light so that it looks like it is **broken**
fractals	describes something that is **broken** into pieces
frail	a **break** in a part of the body
fraction	being easily **broken** or destroyed

Greek and Latin Roots © 2004 Creative Teaching Press

Read-Around Review: frail, fract, frag

I have the first card.
Who has the roots that mean **break?**

I have the roots **frail, fract,** and **frag.**
Who has the word that identifies an incomplete sentence that needs to be revised?

I have the word **fragment.**
Who has the word that names a **break** in part of the body such as the foot?

I have the word **fracture.**
Who has the word that labels a rule that is **broken?**

I have the word **infraction.**
Who has the word that describes the state of being easily **broken** or destroyed?

I have the word **frail.**
Who has the word that describes something that is **broken** into different pieces?

I have the word **fragmented.**
Who has the word that describes a fine china plate that is from the early 1900s and cannot be replaced?

I have the word **fragile.**
Who has the word that describes a part of a whole or a **broken** piece from something?

I have the word **fraction.**
Who has the word that names the ability to have your say in an issue, **break** into the race, and vote?

I have the word **suffrage.**
Who has the word that describes what light does when it bends?

I have the word **refracts.**
Who has the word that describes the type of geometry that creates **broken** patterns out of a smaller version of a design?

I have the word **fractals.**
Who has the first card?

Greek and Latin Roots © 2004 Creative Teaching Press

Vocabulary Quiz: frail, fract, frag

Shade in the bubble for the correct word.

Ⓐ Ⓑ Ⓒ Ⓓ   **1.** This is what people get punished for.
         A) infractions   **B)** fractions   **C)** fractals   **D)** fractures

Ⓐ Ⓑ Ⓒ Ⓓ   **2.** This word is usually used to describe when something is easily broken or destroyed.
         A) fragmented   **B)** suffrage   **C)** refracted   **D)** frail

Ⓐ Ⓑ Ⓒ Ⓓ   **3.** If a vase falls onto the floor and breaks into little pieces, what can you then call the vase?
         A) fragile   **B)** fragmented   **C)** infringed   **D)** refracted

Ⓐ Ⓑ Ⓒ Ⓓ   **4.** Every teacher reminds the students not to use run-ons or these in their writing.
         A) fragments   **B)** suffrage   **C)** frails   **D)** fractions

Ⓐ Ⓑ Ⓒ Ⓓ   **5.** These designs are created by waves pounding on the seashore.
         A) refracted   **B)** fractals   **C)** sufferaged   **D)** fragmented

Ⓐ Ⓑ Ⓒ Ⓓ   **6.** If you break your arm, it could be one of these.
         A) fracture   **B)** fragment   **C)** fraction   **D)** frail

Ⓐ Ⓑ Ⓒ Ⓓ   **7.** Many stores have warning labels near items that are like this, since you will have to buy it if you break it.
         A) fragile   **B)** frail   **C)** suffrage   **D)** fractions

Ⓐ Ⓑ Ⓒ Ⓓ   **8.** If you put a pencil in a cup of water, it will look as if your pencil is broken. What caused that?
         A) fragments   **B)** refraction   **C)** fragile   **D)** suffrage

Ⓐ Ⓑ Ⓒ Ⓓ   **9.** It was a historic moment when women earned the right to this.
         A) suffrage   **B)** fragments   **C)** fractions   **D)** frailty

Ⓐ Ⓑ Ⓒ Ⓓ   **10.** This is another form of a decimal, which is always less than a whole.
         A) fraction   **B)** fragment   **C)** fragile   **D)** suffrage

Write the correct word on the line so the sentence makes sense.

11. Most expensive plates and cups are very _____.

12. Your sentence is missing a subject, so it is only a _____.

13. Dr. Bock said, "You have _____ your leg, so you won't be playing football for many weeks."

14. When you misbehave at school, you may commit an _____.

15. Would you rather eat a whole giant cookie or a _____ of a cookie?

Greek and Latin Roots © 2004 Creative Teaching Press

Review Test: flect, flex and frail, fract, frag

Shade in the bubble for the correct word.

Ⓐ Ⓑ Ⓒ Ⓓ   **1.** If a birthday cake is cut into twenty pieces, what will your slice be compared to the whole cake?
A) fraction   **B)** infringed   **C)** flexible   **D)** frail

Ⓐ Ⓑ Ⓒ Ⓓ   **2.** Which word describes people who can bend all the way down to touch their toes while standing or sitting down?
A) inflexible   **B)** refracting   **C)** flexible   **D)** circumflexed

Ⓐ Ⓑ Ⓒ Ⓓ   **3.** The 100-year-old porcelain doll that was your great grandmother's would probably be described with which of the following words?
A) fragmented   **B)** flexible   **C)** suffrage   **D)** fragile

Ⓐ Ⓑ Ⓒ Ⓓ   **4.** There was a movement by women to win the ability to vote. What was it called?
A) retroflex   **B)** infraction   **C)** flexor   **D)** suffrage

Ⓐ Ⓑ Ⓒ Ⓓ   **5.** If you break a bone in your body, then you will likely be told by a doctor that you have done this to the bone.
A) refracted   **B)** fractured   **C)** deflected   **D)** flexed

Ⓐ Ⓑ Ⓒ Ⓓ   **6.** If you draw a tree beginning with a large Y, then add smaller and smaller Y's, you are creating these.
A) fragmented   **B)** fractals   **C)** flexed   **D)** deflected

Ⓐ Ⓑ Ⓒ Ⓓ   **7.** A mosaic piece of art could be described as this since it's made out of broken pieces of glass or pottery.
A) flexible   **B)** refracted   **C)** fractured   **D)** fragmented

Ⓐ Ⓑ Ⓒ Ⓓ   **8.** What do you see in the mirror due to the bending of light back at you?
A) reflection   **B)** fracture   **C)** deflection   **D)** inflection

Ⓐ Ⓑ Ⓒ Ⓓ   **9.** Elderly people may be described as being in this state since their bones are fragile and their skin is thin.
A) frail   **B)** fragile   **C)** reflected   **D)** flexible

Ⓐ Ⓑ Ⓒ Ⓓ   **10.** What does the root **fract** mean?
A) bend   **B)** break, shatter   **C)** to cut   **D)** to write

Ⓐ Ⓑ Ⓒ Ⓓ   **11.** What does the root **flect** mean?
A) bend   **B)** break   **C)** to cut   **D)** to write

Ⓐ Ⓑ Ⓒ Ⓓ   ***12.** What does **circum** mean in the word *circumflex*?
A) around   **B)** through   **C)** together   **D)** across

Ⓐ Ⓑ Ⓒ Ⓓ   ***13.** What does **re** mean in the words *refract* and *reflection*?
A) again   **B)** within   **C)** after   **D)** outside

Ⓐ Ⓑ Ⓒ Ⓓ   **14.** Finish this analogy: bendable : not bendable :: _____ : _____
A) inflexible : flexible   **B)** flex : flexor
C) reflect : reflection   **D)** flexible : inflexible

Ⓐ Ⓑ Ⓒ Ⓓ   **15.** When people break a rule they may commit this.
A) infraction   **B)** fracture   **C)** frail   **D)** deflection

Word List: junct, join, jug = to join, meet, or link

Vocabulary	Definitions
conjoined (adj)	**joined** together; combined; united
conjugate (v)	to **join** together or match a correct verb in grammar
conjunction (n)	a word that **joins** two phrases or sentences
disjointed (adj)	not **connected;** having no flow in thinking
join (v)	to get together or **meet;** to become included
joint (n)	a place or part of the body where two bones **join** together, usually so they can move
joint committee (n)	a committee with members from both the Senate and the House of Representatives who **join** together and meet to discuss issues
jugular (n)	a vein that carries blood back to the heart from the head; a vein that **joins** the head and the heart
junction (n)	the place where two highways or two sets of railroad tracks cross or **join**
rejoin (v)	to **meet** or get together again

Greek and Latin Roots © 2004 Creative Teaching Press

Vocabulary Sort: junct, join, jug

conjunction	to **meet** or get together again
disjointed	a vein that carries blood back to the heart from the head; a vein that **joins** the head and the heart
jugular	to get together or **meet;** to become included
junction	a committee with members from both the Senate and the House of Representatives who **join** together and meet to discuss issues
join	the place where two highways or two sets of railroad tracks cross or **join**
conjoined	a place or part of the body where two bones **join** together, usually so they can move
joint	to **join** together or match a correct verb in grammar
conjugate	**joined** together; combined; united
joint committee	not **connected;** having no flow in thinking
rejoin	a word that **joins** two phrases or sentences

Greek and Latin Roots © 2004 Creative Teaching Press

Read-Around Review: junct, join, jug

I have the first card.
Who has the roots that mean **join, meet,** or **link?**

I have the roots **junct, join,** and **jug.**
Who has the word that describes a place on a railroad where the tracks **join** together?

I have the word **junction.**
Who has the word that names the vein that **joins** the head and the heart?

I have the word **jugular.**
Who has the word that describes something that is not connected or doesn't make any sense?

I have the word **disjointed.**
Who has the word that explains what you do when you **meet** up with someone?

I have the word **join.**
Who has the word that describes things that are connected together or combined?

I have the word **conjoined.**
Who has the word that names a word in a sentence that combines or **joins** other words or phrases into one sentence?

I have the word **conjunction.**
Who has the word that describes what you are doing when you **meet** up with someone again at a later time?

I have the word **rejoin.**
Who has the name of the group that represents members from both the Senate and the House of Representatives in United States government?

I have the words **joint committee.**
Who has the word that labels a body part at which two bones come together so they can move?

I have the word **joint.**
Who has the word that names listing all the forms of a verb?

I have the word **conjugate.**
Who has the first card?

Greek and Latin Roots © 2004 Creative Teaching Press

Name _____   Date _____

Vocabulary Quiz: junct, join, jug

Shade in the bubble for the correct word.

Ⓐ Ⓑ Ⓒ Ⓓ   **1.** What do people do when they decide that they want to be in the Boy or Girl Scouts, PTA, or a club at the school?
   A) join   **B)** junction   **C)** conjugate   **D)** jugular

Ⓐ Ⓑ Ⓒ Ⓓ   **2.** Name the vein that joins a person's head to the heart.
   A) junction   **B)** rejoin   **C)** conjoined   **D)** jugular

Ⓐ Ⓑ Ⓒ Ⓓ   **3.** What type of words are *but, therefore, thus, so,* and *however*?
   A) rejoined   **B)** conjunctions   **C)** conjugates   **D)** disjointed

Ⓐ Ⓑ Ⓒ Ⓓ   **4.** Which word names a place in your body where two bones join together?
   A) junction   **B)** joint   **C)** rejoin   **D)** conjugate

Ⓐ Ⓑ Ⓒ Ⓓ   **5.** If you dropped out of the Cleanup Committee, then decided that they needed you, what did you likely do?
   A) rejoined   **B)** conjugated   **C)** disjointed   **D)** jugular

Ⓐ Ⓑ Ⓒ Ⓓ   **6.** If a discussion was going on with representatives and senators in the same group, what might the group be called?
   A) joined   **B)** rejoined   **C)** disjointed   **D)** joint committee

Ⓐ Ⓑ Ⓒ Ⓓ   **7.** When learning another language, it's important to learn how to do this so that you don't sound silly when you speak.
   A) conjugate   **B)** disjointed   **C)** jugular   **D)** conjoin

Ⓐ Ⓑ Ⓒ Ⓓ   **8.** What is the location called where highways cross or join together?
   A) junction   **B)** rejoin   **C)** conjugate   **D)** joint

Ⓐ Ⓑ Ⓒ Ⓓ   **9.** When giving a speech, it's important to make sure the sentences have a natural flow so the speech doesn't sound _____.
   A) conjoined   **B)** conjugated   **C)** rejoined   **D)** disjointed

Ⓐ Ⓑ Ⓒ Ⓓ   **10.** If twins are born connected to each other, what are they called?
   A) jugular   **B)** conjugated   **C)** conjoined   **D)** disjointed

Write the correct word on the line so the sentence makes sense.

11. Please combine these two short sentences into one using a _____.

12. You can feel your pulse if you put your finger on the _____ vein.

13. "I'll meet you at the _____ where the Birmingham train meets the Devonshire train."

14. If a science fiction story talks about inventions, magical potions, and real-life television stars, then it will sound very _____.

15. "Do you want to _____ the cast as the lead character? I have an extra script," said Ms. Kominsky.

Greek and Latin Roots © 2004 Creative Teaching Press

Word List: rupt = break

Vocabulary	Definitions
abrupt (adj)	sudden; unexpected; **broken** into what is expected
bankrupt (adj)	to be out of money; financially ruined; to "**break** the bank"
corrupt (adj)	evil; dishonest; to **break** away from honesty
corruptible (adj)	able to be influenced into doing something that **breaks** away from the rules; able to become bad
disrupt (v)	to **break** up; to cause confusion
disruption (n)	something that **breaks** someone's concentration; bothersome; annoying
erupt (v)	to explode; to **break** out with force
interrupt (v)	to **break** into someone's conversation
interruption (n)	something that **breaks** up what you were doing; an unplanned event that **breaks** up an activity
rupture (v)	to burst or **break** open (usually a body part)

Greek and Latin Roots © 2004 Creative Teaching Press

Vocabulary Sort: rupt

corrupt	to be out of money; financially ruined; to "**break** the bank"
interruption	to explode; to **break** out with force
disrupt	to burst or **break** open (usually a body part)
erupt	to **break** up; to cause confusion
corruptible	sudden; unexpected; **broken** into what is expected
rupture	to **break** into someone's conversation
interrupt	something that **breaks** up what you were doing; an unplanned event that **breaks** up an activity
disruption	able to be influenced into doing something that **breaks** away from the rules; able to become bad
abrupt	something that **breaks** someone's concentration; bothersome; annoying
bankrupt	evil; dishonest; to **break** away from honesty

Greek and Latin Roots © 2004 Creative Teaching Press

Read-Around Review: rupt

I have the first card.
Who has the root that means to **break?**

I have the root **rupt.**
Who has the word that describes what you do when you **break** in on someone's conversation?

I have the word **interrupt.**
Who has the word that describes what the volcano does as lava bursts out of it?

I have the word **erupts.**
Who has the word that names what a person who makes silly noises in class creates?

I have the word **disruption.**
Who has the word that names what you will be if you lose all of the money you have saved?

I have the word **bankrupt.**
Who has the word that describes a person who could easily be talked into doing something that is against the law?

I have the word **corruptible.**
Who has the word that describes what happens to an organ or a tissue in the body when it suddenly bursts open and you must have surgery?

I have the word **rupture.**
Who has the word that describes what a bad person tries to do to a good person to make him or her misbehave?

I have the word **corrupt.**
Who has the word that describes a noise or comment that **breaks** up your "train of thought" or takes you away from what you are doing?

I have the word **interruption.**
Who has the word that describes what a class clown does to the rest of the class while they are trying to learn which explains why he or she is often punished?

I have the word **disrupts.**
Who has the word that describes a sudden change?

I have the word **abrupt.**
Who has the first card?

Greek and Latin Roots © 2004 Creative Teaching Press

Vocabulary Quiz: rupt

Shade in the bubble for the correct word.

Ⓐ Ⓑ Ⓒ Ⓓ   **1.** If this word describes a child, then the chances are good that the child is often in trouble.
   A) erupting   **B)** ruptured   **C)** bankrupt   **D)** disruptive

Ⓐ Ⓑ Ⓒ Ⓓ   **2.** What do volcanoes do as lava shoots out of the cone from deep within the core of the earth?
   A) rupture   **B)** erupt   **C)** interrupt   **D)** corrupt

Ⓐ Ⓑ Ⓒ Ⓓ   **3.** An honest child will not be this.
   A) bankrupt   **B)** ruptures   **C)** corruptible   **D)** abrupt

Ⓐ Ⓑ Ⓒ Ⓓ   **4.** Try not to do this to your parents while they are talking to you.
   A) interrupt   **B)** corrupt   **C)** erupt   **D)** rupture

Ⓐ Ⓑ Ⓒ Ⓓ   **5.** If this happens to your appendix, it could be deadly.
   A) rupture   **B)** corrupt   **C)** erupt   **D)** disrupt

Ⓐ Ⓑ Ⓒ Ⓓ   **6.** One day a cockroach ran through the classroom! Wow! It really did what to the class?
   A) disrupted   **B)** corrupted   **C)** bankrupted   **D)** ruptured

Ⓐ Ⓑ Ⓒ Ⓓ   **7.** Some people who end up in jail are punished for being this.
   A) interrupted   **B)** erupted   **C)** ruptured   **D)** corrupt

Ⓐ Ⓑ Ⓒ Ⓓ   **8.** Learning to save while you're young will help make sure that you don't end up like this one day.
   A) corrupt   **B)** bankrupt   **C)** erupted   **D)** ruptured

Ⓐ Ⓑ Ⓒ Ⓓ   **9.** Our reading lesson came to an _____ end when the fire alarm went off.
   A) abrupt   **B)** corrupt   **C)** erupted   **D)** ruptured

Ⓐ Ⓑ Ⓒ Ⓓ   **10.** A voice from the loudspeaker said, "Sorry for the _____, but will the owner of the black car please move it from the fire zone immediately?"
   A) corruption   **B)** abrupt   **C)** interruption   **D)** rupture

Write the correct word on the line so the sentence makes sense.

11. If you scream in a person's ear, it can cause a _____ ear drum.

12. Many people feel that commercials _____ their favorite television shows.

13. Do not let other people _____ you. Stay honest!

14. The Planetary Problems show featured the _____ of three volcanoes.

15. The unruly student created a _____ and was quickly sent to the principal's office.

Greek and Latin Roots © 2004 Creative Teaching Press

Review Test: junct, join, jug and rupt

Shade in the bubble for the correct word.

Ⓐ Ⓑ Ⓒ Ⓓ   **1.** While driving, some people have to make sudden stops when they see things in the road that shouldn't be there. What type of stops do they make?
A) disjointed   **B)** junction   **C)** disruptive   **D)** abrupt

Ⓐ Ⓑ Ⓒ Ⓓ   **2.** When you see lava burst out of the volcano, what are you seeing the lava do?
A) disrupt   **B)** erupt   **C)** junction   **D)** rupture

Ⓐ Ⓑ Ⓒ Ⓓ   **3.** What is the name of the word that links ideas, phrases, or sentences within a sentence?
A) conjunction   **B)** interruption   **C)** junction   **D)** conjugate

Ⓐ Ⓑ Ⓒ Ⓓ   **4.** When people owe much more money then they have, sometimes they become _____.
A) corrupt   **B)** bankrupt   **C)** disjointed   **D)** conjoined

Ⓐ Ⓑ Ⓒ Ⓓ   **5.** If a person is easily talked into doing something that she knows is wrong, which word describes her?
A) conjugate   **B)** disruptive   **C)** interrupted   **D)** corruptible

Ⓐ Ⓑ Ⓒ Ⓓ   **6.** When you plan to meet your friend from another class at lunch, what will you do with him?
A) disrupt   **B)** interrupt   **C)** join   **D)** corrupt

Ⓐ Ⓑ Ⓒ Ⓓ   **7.** If an organ inside of the human body does this, then the person will need to see the doctor immediately.
A) ruptures   **B)** disjoints   **C)** corrupts   **D)** erupts

Ⓐ Ⓑ Ⓒ Ⓓ   **8.** What is the name of the vein that carries blood from the head back to the heart?
A) jugular   **B)** disrupted   **C)** joint committee **D)** junction

Ⓐ Ⓑ Ⓒ Ⓓ   **9.** Children in classrooms who create these are often sent out.
A) disruptions   **B)** eruptions   **C)** conjugates   **D)** junctions

Ⓐ Ⓑ Ⓒ Ⓓ   **10.** What does the root **rupt** mean?
A) to break   **B)** to throw   **C)** to cut   **D)** to join

Ⓐ Ⓑ Ⓒ Ⓓ   **11.** What does the root **junct** mean?
A) to break   **B)** to throw   **C)** to cut   **D)** to join

Ⓐ Ⓑ Ⓒ Ⓓ   ***12.** What does **dis** mean in the words *disruptive* and *disjointed*?
A) not   **B)** break   **C)** join   **D)** across

Ⓐ Ⓑ Ⓒ Ⓓ   ***13.** What does **inter** mean in the word *interrupt*?
A) between   **B)** within   **C)** after   **D)** outside

Ⓐ Ⓑ Ⓒ Ⓓ   **14.** If you cut in on someone's conversation without being asked to join in, what have you done?
A) interrupted   **B)** conjoined   **C)** joined   **D)** ruptured

Ⓐ Ⓑ Ⓒ Ⓓ   **15.** Which word describes what you do when you join a verb and a noun together?
A) erupt   **B)** disrupt   **C)** conjoin   **D)** conjugate

Greek and Latin Roots © 2004 Creative Teaching Press

Word List: cede, ceed, cess = go; yield

Vocabulary	Definitions
accessible (adj)	able to **go** in to, enter, or approach
accessory (n)	an article or item worn with an outfit that "**goes** with" or matches the outfit
concede (v)	to **yield** to an opponent that one has lost; to give in; to admit that something is true and valid
exceed (v)	to **go** or be beyond the limit or expectations
intercede (v)	to mediate; to **go** between people to help them reach an agreement
precede (v)	to **go** before something else in time, order, place, or rank
proceed (v)	to keep on **going;** to **go** ahead with something; to move along
recede (v)	to **go** or move back
recess (n)	the time during which people **go** out to take a break
successor (n)	a person who **goes** after someone else (usually related to a person taking over a job that is of higher rank)

Vocabulary Sort: cede, ceed, cess

exceed	to **go** before something else in time, order, place, or rank
proceed	the time during which people **go** out to take a break
recede	to **yield** to an opponent that one has lost; to give in; to admit that something is true and valid
accessory	able to **go** in to, enter, or approach
successor	to keep on **going;** to **go** ahead with something; to move along
intercede	a person who **goes** after someone else (usually related to a person taking over someone's job that is of higher rank)
concede	to **go** or move back
recess	an article or item worn with an outfit that "**goes** with" or matches the outfit
precede	to **go** or be beyond the limit or expectations
accessible	to mediate; to **go** between people to help them reach an agreement

Greek and Latin Roots © 2004 Creative Teaching Press

Read-Around Review: cede, ceed, cess

I have the first card.
Who has the roots that mean to **go** or to **yield?**

I have the roots **cede, ceed,** and **cess.**
Who has the word that means that you keep on **going** with something or you **go** ahead with plans?

I have the word **proceed.**
Who has the word that means that you give in and admit that you have lost?

I have the word **concede.**
Who has the word that describes something that someone might wear that **goes** with the rest of the outfit that person is wearing?

I have the word **accessory.**
Who has the word that describes what you do when you do more than is expected or **go** beyond the minimum?

I have the word **exceed.**
Who has the word that identifies the person who **goes** after someone else in a job?

I have the word **successor.**
Who has the word that describes what you do when you help two people get along and settle their differences?

I have the word **intercede.**
Who has the word that names the time when children **go** out and take a break, which usually involves a snack and play time?

I have the word **recess.**
Who has the word that describes what happens when something moves backward?

I have the word **recede.**
Who has the word that describes something that allows people to enter?

I have the word **accessible.**
Who has the word that describes what something does when it **goes** before something else?

I have the word **precedes.**
Who has the first card?

Greek and Latin Roots © 2004 Creative Teaching Press

Name _____   Date _____

Vocabulary Quiz: cede, ceed, cess

Shade in the bubble for the correct word.

Ⓐ Ⓑ Ⓒ Ⓓ **1.** In most states, public buildings must be made with ramps so that people in wheelchairs may enter. That means the buildings are what?
A) intercede   **B)** accessible   **C)** accessories   **D)** proceeded

Ⓐ Ⓑ Ⓒ Ⓓ **2.** In which department would you search for hats and purses as a gift?
A) recess   **B)** intercede   **C)** successor   **D)** accessories

Ⓐ Ⓑ Ⓒ Ⓓ **3.** Hair growth commercials are aimed at people who are worried that their hair will do this.
A) exceed   **B)** concede   **C)** precede   **D)** recede

Ⓐ Ⓑ Ⓒ Ⓓ **4.** When an election ends, you will usually hear the person who does not win do this.
A) recede   **B)** concede   **C)** recess   **D)** exceed

Ⓐ Ⓑ Ⓒ Ⓓ **5.** People who get to celebrate their 100th birthday do this to the average life span.
A) precede   **B)** recess   **C)** exceed   **D)** proceed

Ⓐ Ⓑ Ⓒ Ⓓ **6.** Although it was raining, the bride and groom decided to go ahead with their wedding. What did they do?
A) proceeded   **B)** recessed   **C)** receded   **D)** preceded

Ⓐ Ⓑ Ⓒ Ⓓ **7.** When the brother and sister were arguing over who had control of the remote control, their mother stepped in to do this.
A) intercede   **B)** recede   **C)** precede   **D)** exceed

Ⓐ Ⓑ Ⓒ Ⓓ **8.** Who will be next to the throne in England? Who will be the _____?
A) receding   **B)** recess   **C)** successor   **D)** predecessor

Ⓐ Ⓑ Ⓒ Ⓓ **9.** Is it time for a break yet? I'm ready for this!
A) recede   **B)** exceeding   **C)** recess   **D)** successors

Ⓐ Ⓑ Ⓒ Ⓓ **10.** At the flag ceremony, the school sings a patriotic song after raising the flag. Therefore, the raising of the flag _____ the song.
A) precedes   **B)** proceeds   **C)** succeeds   **D)** accessible

Write the correct word on the line so the sentence makes sense.

11. The song by Natalie will _____ the awards ceremony. That's a terrific start!

12. Although the morning started with a small earthquake, her plans _____ as usual.

13. The boxer had to _____ that he lost the match.

14. Your parents will be pleased if you _____ their expectations in life!

15. At _____, would you like to play basketball with me?

Greek and Latin Roots © 2004 Creative Teaching Press

Word List: vers, vert = turn

Vocabulary	Definitions
anniversary (n)	the date on which an event occurs every year; every year an event **turns** a year older
conversation (n)	a discussion that switches from one person to another; a discussion that "**turns** back and forth"
convert (v)	to **turn** or change your beliefs or way of thinking
diversify (v)	to divide up money into different investments so that if one area **turns** for the worse then you will be protected
diversion (n)	something that **turns** your attention off of what you are thinking about
extrovert (n)	a person who **turns** his or her attention outward toward other people
introvert (n)	a person who **turns** his or her attention inward toward himself or herself; a shy person
invert (v)	to **turn** or flip in the opposite direction
revert (v)	to **turn** back to a previous action or thought; to go back in thought or speech; to give back
subvert (v)	to corrupt or undermine; to **turn** against established authority

Greek and Latin Roots © 2004 Creative Teaching Press

Vocabulary Sort: vers, vert

extrovert	something that **turns** your attention off of what you are thinking about
diversion	a person who **turns** his or her attention inward toward himself or herself; a shy person
invert	a discussion that switches from one person to another; a discussion that "**turns** back and forth"
convert	to **turn** or flip in the opposite direction
diversify	the date on which an event occurs every year; every year an event **turns** a year older
subvert	to corrupt or undermine; to **turn** against established authority
conversation	to divide up money into different investments so that if one area **turns** for the worse then you will be protected
revert	a person who **turns** his or her attention outward toward other people
anniversary	to **turn** or change your beliefs or way of thinking
introvert	to **turn** back to a previous action or thought; to go back in thought or speech; to give back

Greek and Latin Roots © 2004 Creative Teaching Press

Read-Around Review: vers, vert

I have the first card.
Who has the roots that mean **turn?**

I have the roots **vers** and **vert.**
Who has the word that describes what you do when you change your beliefs or way of thinking?

I have the word **convert.**
Who has the word that identifies the type of people who love being in a crowd since they send their energy outward?

I have the word **extrovert.**
Who has the word that means to **turn** in the opposite direction?

I have the word **invert.**
Who has the word that describes what smart people do with their money so that they won't lose it all with one bad **turn?**

I have the word **diversify.**
Who has the word that identifies the type of people who turn their attention inward, which makes them appear to be very shy?

I have the word **introvert.**
Who has the word that names the date on which an event occurs every year?

I have the word **anniversary.**
Who has the word that identifies a discussion in which the speakers take **turns** talking and listening to each other?

I have the word **conversation.**
Who has the word that names what something could be called if it takes your attention away from what you are trying to focus on?

I have the word **diversion.**
Who has the word that describes what you do when you go back to what you originally thought or you change your mind back?

I have the word **revert.**
Who has the word that describes what some criminals do to authority?

I have the word **subvert.**
Who has the first card?

Greek and Latin Roots © 2004 Creative Teaching Press

Name _____   Date _____

Vocabulary Quiz: vers, vert

Shade in the bubble for the correct word.

Ⓐ Ⓑ Ⓒ Ⓓ   **1.** Taking turns while speaking and listening to another person is a good way to have one of these.
    A) diversion **B)** anniversary **C)** inverse **D)** conversation

Ⓐ Ⓑ Ⓒ Ⓓ   **2.** Any good money manager will recommend that you do this when you are old enough to invest your money.
    A) diversify **B)** convert **C)** subvert **D)** inverse

Ⓐ Ⓑ Ⓒ Ⓓ   **3.** The surprise visit from his Aunt Shanelle was a nice one of these, since Cameron was beginning to worry too much about his upcoming trip.
    A) diversion **B)** inverse **C)** subvert **D)** introvert

Ⓐ Ⓑ Ⓒ Ⓓ   **4.** What type of person are you if you love to give and get attention from other people?
    A) introvert **B)** convert **C)** revert **D)** extrovert

Ⓐ Ⓑ Ⓒ Ⓓ   **5.** When you flip a switch from on to off you do this to it.
    A) convert **B)** extrovert **C)** invert **D)** subversive

Ⓐ Ⓑ Ⓒ Ⓓ   **6.** People with this type of personality may be very quiet at school.
    A) introvert **B)** extrovert **C)** convert **D)** inverse

Ⓐ Ⓑ Ⓒ Ⓓ   **7.** People who are not honest and good may try to do this to the law.
    A) subvert **B)** inverse **C)** revert **D)** convert

Ⓐ Ⓑ Ⓒ Ⓓ   **8.** This is what some people do at churches.
    A) revert **B)** subvert **C)** inverse **D)** convert

Ⓐ Ⓑ Ⓒ Ⓓ   **9.** Every May 24th the couple celebrates the remembrance of their wedding. What is this called?
    A) inverse **B)** anniversary **C)** introvert **D)** reverted

Ⓐ Ⓑ Ⓒ Ⓓ   **10.** "It's time to _____ back to my original thought!"
    A) revert **B)** subvert **C)** introvert **D)** convert

Write the correct word on the line so the sentence makes sense.

11. The people who love to be in talent shows, crack jokes, and be the center of attention are usually the _____ in the room.

12. When Alex goes home, he likes to read or draw by himself. He may be a(n) _____.

13. My parents look forward to celebrating their _____ each year.

14. Jeff's telephone _____ was interrupted by the doorbell.

15. While studying, any _____ could be a problem.

Greek and Latin Roots © 2004 Creative Teaching Press

Name _____ Date _____

Review Test: cede, ceed, cess and vers, vert

Shade in the bubble for the correct word.

Ⓐ Ⓑ Ⓒ Ⓓ **1.** Emma wants to be an actress or a singer when she grows up. She's always loved being in front of the audience. Which word describes Emma the best?
A) introvert   **B)** diversified   **C)** divergent   **D)** extrovert

Ⓐ Ⓑ Ⓒ Ⓓ **2.** A king who takes the place of another king when he dies is called what?
A) successor   **B)** revert   **C)** extrovert   **D)** accessory

Ⓐ Ⓑ Ⓒ Ⓓ **3.** The owner placed a cat door on the back door of the house. What did this make the house for the cat?
A) accessory   **B)** accessible   **C)** inverted   **D)** subverted

Ⓐ Ⓑ Ⓒ Ⓓ **4.** Dentists remind everyone to brush often and floss daily to keep the gum line from beginning to do what?
A) exceed   **B)** recede   **C)** concede   **D)** recess

Ⓐ Ⓑ Ⓒ Ⓓ **5.** The presidential election was so close! Finally, the person who lost did this.
A) receded   **B)** diversified   **C)** conceded   **D)** interceded

Ⓐ Ⓑ Ⓒ Ⓓ **6.** When dogs get groomed, the shampooing usually comes before the blow drying. One might say the shampooing _____ the blow drying.
A) intercedes   **B)** proceeds   **C)** concedes   **D)** precedes

Ⓐ Ⓑ Ⓒ Ⓓ **7.** Kendra wants to travel to Europe. First, she must do this with her United States dollars so she will have the correct form of money.
A) revert   **B)** convert   **C)** exceed   **D)** subvert

Ⓐ Ⓑ Ⓒ Ⓓ **8.** A purse, shoes, or a bracelet would be considered these.
A) accessories   **B)** introverts   **C)** diversions   **D)** recess

Ⓐ Ⓑ Ⓒ Ⓓ **9.** When people worry about things, sometimes one of these is welcome so they take their mind off of their worries.
A) diversion   **B)** accessory   **C)** intercede   **D)** revert

Ⓐ Ⓑ Ⓒ Ⓓ **10.** What do the roots **vers** and **vert** mean?
A) to turn   **B)** to throw   **C)** to go   **D)** to cut

Ⓐ Ⓑ Ⓒ Ⓓ **11.** What do the roots **ceed** and **cede** mean?
A) to turn   **B)** to throw   **C)** to go   **D)** to cut

Ⓐ Ⓑ Ⓒ Ⓓ ***12.** What does **ex** mean in the word *extrovert*?
A) in   **B)** out   **C)** together   **D)** apart

Ⓐ Ⓑ Ⓒ Ⓓ ***13.** What does **sub** mean in the word *subvert*?
A) over   **B)** within   **C)** after   **D)** under

Ⓐ Ⓑ Ⓒ Ⓓ ***14.** What does **pre** mean in the word *precede*?
A) after   **B)** before   **C)** apart   **D)** follow

Ⓐ Ⓑ Ⓒ Ⓓ **15.** Which word describes what you do if you go ahead with plans even though something may have gotten in the way?
A) recede   **B)** proceed   **C)** diversify   **D)** revert

Greek and Latin Roots © 2004 Creative Teaching Press

Word List: tract = pull

Vocabulary	Definitions
abstract (adj)	**pulled** away from direct relation to anything; impersonal as in attitude or views
attract (v)	to **pull** into something; to **pull** into oneself
contract (v)	to **pull** together to make smaller in size or bulk; to **pull** inward; opposite of "expand"
distract (v)	to **pull** a person's attention in another direction
extract (v)	to **pull** out by force
protract (v)	to **pull** out; to make something take longer; to prolong
retraction (n)	a statement or promise that is **pulled** back or taken back
subtract (v)	to **pull** some out, therefore having less left over
traction (n)	a **pull** to the arm or leg muscles to bring a bone back into place when it is dislocated or fractured
tractor (n)	a powerful vehicle that **pulls** farm machines and hauls heavy loads

Greek and Latin Roots © 2004 Creative Teaching Press

Vocabulary Sort: tract

distract	to **pull** out by force
retraction	to **pull** together to make smaller in size or bulk; to **pull** inward; opposite of "expand"
attract	to **pull** some out, therefore having less left over
traction	a **pull** to the arm or leg muscles to bring a bone back into place when it is dislocated or fractured
contract	**pulled** away from direct relation to anything; impersonal as in attitude or views
protract	a statement or promise that is **pulled** back or taken back
abstract	to **pull** out; to make something take longer; to prolong
subtract	to **pull** into something; to **pull** into oneself
tractor	to **pull** a person's attention in another direction
extract	a powerful vehicle that **pulls** farm machines and hauls heavy loads

Greek and Latin Roots © 2004 Creative Teaching Press

Read-Around Review: tract

I have the first card.
Who has the root that means **pull?**

I have the root **tract.**
Who has the word that identifies a vehicle that **pulls** heavy loads?

I have the word **tractor.**
Who has the word that describes what a magnet does when it **pulls** a magnetic object close to it?

I have the word **attract.**
Who has the word that describes what you are doing when you **pull** someone's attention away from what he is working on?

I have the word **distract.**
Who has the word that describes what your legs are in when they are being **pulled** back in the hope of popping the bones back into the proper place?

I have the word **traction.**
Who has the word that describes what you are doing when you **pull** something out by force?

I have the word **extract.**
Who has the word that describes what you do when you **pull** something out and make it take longer?

I have the word **protract.**
Who has the word that names a statement that people write to take back something that they said or wrote?

I have the word **retraction.**
Who has the word that describes a thought that doesn't seem to be directly related to anything?

I have the word **abstract.**
Who has the word that is the opposite of "expand" and means that you **pull** something inward to make it smaller?

I have the word **contract.**
Who has the word that describes what you do when you take a piece of candy away from two other pieces of candy?

I have the word **subtract.**
Who has the first card?

Greek and Latin Roots © 2004 Creative Teaching Press

Vocabulary Quiz: tract

Shade in the bubble for the correct word.

Ⓐ Ⓑ Ⓒ Ⓓ **1.** The magazine agreed to print this, since the man was sorry that he made his comment in the first place.
A) protract **B)** attraction **C)** abstract **D)** retraction

Ⓐ Ⓑ Ⓒ Ⓓ **2.** "I'm sorry. I'll have to remove your tooth, Denise." What is Dr. Harrison about to do to her tooth?
A) retract **B)** protract **C)** attract **D)** extract

Ⓐ Ⓑ Ⓒ Ⓓ **3.** "Let me help you drive that vehicle to haul the cement," said Troy. What type of vehicle is Troy referring to?
A) tractor **B)** traction **C)** distract **D)** abstract

Ⓐ Ⓑ Ⓒ Ⓓ **4.** Newton's leg was connected to a metal bar and held in the air as the doctor tried to move the bone back into place. What was his leg in?
A) traction **B)** contract **C)** attraction **D)** protractor

Ⓐ Ⓑ Ⓒ Ⓓ **5.** You were paid $10.00. You owe your sister $5.00. What would you do to get the total amount of money you have left?
A) contract **B)** attract **C)** retract **D)** subtract

Ⓐ Ⓑ Ⓒ Ⓓ **6.** When ice is frozen it will do this. When it thaws, it will expand.
A) abstract **B)** protract **C)** contract **D)** distract

Ⓐ Ⓑ Ⓒ Ⓓ **7.** Try not to do this to the vet when he is giving your pet a shot.
A) distract **B)** retract **C)** attract **D)** protract

Ⓐ Ⓑ Ⓒ Ⓓ **8.** Did you know that certain colors will grab your attention more than others? These are colors that do what to you?
A) distract **B)** attract **C)** protract **D)** abstract

Ⓐ Ⓑ Ⓒ Ⓓ **9.** Do you have to make it take so long? You're doing this!
A) protracting **B)** contracting **C)** attracting **D)** abstracting

Ⓐ Ⓑ Ⓒ Ⓓ **10.** This type of art is usually so unique that only the artist really knows what she painted.
A) attractive **B)** distracting **C)** abstract **D)** contract

Write the correct word on the line so the sentence makes sense.

11. When you pull in your breath, then your stomach will _____.

12. If you _____ someone in class, then he or she won't be able to complete the required work.

13. The newspaper printed the _____, since the information in yesterday's paper was actually not correct.

14. The Pet Protectors Club tries to _____ members who are animal lovers.

15. What kind of _____ drawing is that? I can't tell if it's a banana or a horse!

Greek and Latin Roots © 2004 Creative Teaching Press

Word List: struct = build

Vocabulary	Definitions
construction (n)	what is **built; buildings** that are created or produced
destruction (n)	the act of taking down or destroying something that was **built**
infrastructure (n)	the parts of a city on which the rest of the city was **built** around: roads, communication, transportation, and schools
instruct (v)	to **build** knowledge
instructor (n)	a person who helps someone **build** knowledge
misconstrue (v)	to **build** the wrong meaning; to misunderstand; to interpret the wrong way
obstruction (n)	something that blocks the way of things being created or **built;** something in the way
reconstruct (v)	to **build** again
substructure (n)	the base, support, or foundation of a **building**
superstructure (n)	something **built** on top of something else; the part of the **building** that was **built** on top of the foundation or base

Greek and Latin Roots © 2004 Creative Teaching Press

Vocabulary Sort: struct

destruction	to **build** again
instruct	something **built** on top of something else; the part of the **building** that was **built** on top of the foundation or base
reconstruct	to **build** the wrong meaning; to misunderstand; to interpret the wrong way
obstruction	the base, support, or foundation of a **building**
misconstrue	the parts of a city on which the rest of the city was **built** around: roads, communication, transportation, and schools
substructure	something that blocks the way of things being created or **built;** something in the way
infrastructure	to **build** knowledge
superstructure	a person who helps someone **build** knowledge
instructor	what is **built; buildings** that are created or produced
construction	the act of taking down or destroying something that was **built**

Greek and Latin Roots © 2004 Creative Teaching Press

Read-Around Review: struct

I have the first card.
Who has the root that means **build?**

I have the root **struct.**
Who has the word that describes what you do when you **build** something again?

I have the word **reconstruct.**
Who has the word that names the act of tearing down what was **built?**

I have the word **destruction.**
Who has the word that means to **build** the wrong meaning, to misunderstand, or to interpret the wrong way?

I have the word **misconstrue.**
Who has the word that describes something that is in the way of **building** or creating?

I have the word **obstruction.**
Who has the word that names the person who tries to help students **build** knowledge?

I have the word **instructor.**
Who has the word that names the parts within a city that help the city survive and continue **building,** including the roads and lines of communication?

I have the word **infrastructure.**
Who has the word that names what a teacher does?

I have the word **instruct.**
Who has the word that names the work of the person who **builds** homes?

I have the word **construction.**
Who has the word that names the part of a **building** that was created on top of another part?

I have the word **superstructure.**
Who has the word that labels the base or foundation of a structure being **built?**

I have the word **substructure.**
Who has the first card?

Greek and Latin Roots © 2004 Creative Teaching Press

Name _____   Date _____

Vocabulary Quiz: struct

Shade in the bubble for the correct word.

Ⓐ Ⓑ Ⓒ Ⓓ   **1.** After an earthquake or other natural disaster, what do people need to do to their homes?
A) superstructure   **B)** reconstruct   **C)** misconstrue   **D)** obstruct

Ⓐ Ⓑ Ⓒ Ⓓ   **2.** Your teacher is also known as this, since he or she builds your knowledge about math, reading, science, and history.
A) instructor   **B)** substructure   **C)** destructor   **D)** obstruction

Ⓐ Ⓑ Ⓒ Ⓓ   **3.** Something that stands in your way could be called what?
A) construction   **B)** destruction   **C)** obstruction   **D)** instruct

Ⓐ Ⓑ Ⓒ Ⓓ   **4.** What is another word for misunderstanding something?
A) misconstrue   **B)** instruct   **C)** construction   **D)** destructive

Ⓐ Ⓑ Ⓒ Ⓓ   **5.** The structures within a building site that are often not even seen are part of what?
A) infrastructure   **B)** destruction   **C)** instruct   **D)** substructure

Ⓐ Ⓑ Ⓒ Ⓓ   **6.** A flood can wash away an entire town, creating this on a massive scale.
A) destruction   **B)** construction   **C)** instruction   **D)** superstructure

Ⓐ Ⓑ Ⓒ Ⓓ   **7.** What do you call something that is built on top of something else?
A) superstructure   **B)** substructure   **C)** instructor   **D)** destruction

Ⓐ Ⓑ Ⓒ Ⓓ   **8.** You are in school to learn from this.
A) instruction   **B)** construction   **C)** reconstruction   **D)** destruction

Ⓐ Ⓑ Ⓒ Ⓓ   **9.** This form of work involves building homes and office buildings.
A) destruction   **B)** construction   **C)** substructures   **D)** instruction

Ⓐ Ⓑ Ⓒ Ⓓ   **10.** Some homes have basements, which may be considered to be these.
A) superstructures   **B)** substructures   **C)** instructors   **D)** obstructions

Write the correct word on the line so the sentence makes sense.

11. Most _____ companies use bulldozers and cranes.

12. After the river overflowed, some people along the river bank had to _____ their homes because of the terrible water damage.

13. She _____ my comments. I didn't mean that. She simply did not understand what I was trying to say.

14. On law-related television shows, you will sometimes hear the term "_____ of justice" when a person stands in the way of the police upholding the law.

15. Natural disasters can cause widespread _____.

Greek and Latin Roots © 2004 Creative Teaching Press

Review Test: tract and struct

Shade in the bubble for the correct word.

Ⓐ Ⓑ Ⓒ Ⓓ **1.** "Hey! We need to stop watching the crow dig in the trash can. It's keeping us from studying!" What was the crow?
   A) distraction   **B)** protraction   **C)** instructor   **D)** contracting

Ⓐ Ⓑ Ⓒ Ⓓ **2.** The hurricane ruined the front porch, so the family will need to do this to it.
   A) construct   **B)** reconstruct   **C)** attract   **D)** protract

Ⓐ Ⓑ Ⓒ Ⓓ **3.** Have you seen the commercial for the juice machine that gets every last drop out of the lemons for fresh lemonade? What is the machine called?
   A) protractor   **B)** contractor   **C)** destructor   **D)** extractor

Ⓐ Ⓑ Ⓒ Ⓓ **4.** Did you know that the color yellow does this to bees?
   A) attracts   **B)** contracts   **C)** obstructs   **D)** destructs

Ⓐ Ⓑ Ⓒ Ⓓ **5.** If you do not understand what someone's tone of voice means, you can _____ what she is saying.
   A) instruction   **B)** contraction   **C)** retract   **D)** misconstrue

Ⓐ Ⓑ Ⓒ Ⓓ **6.** The broken-down car in the middle of the highway was definitely one of these to the drivers.
   A) obstruction   **B)** construction   **C)** tractor   **D)** retraction

Ⓐ Ⓑ Ⓒ Ⓓ **7.** Mr. Lopez bought a new more powerful _____ to haul heavy loads for his farming business.
   A) attraction   **B)** tractor   **C)** construction   **D)** extract

Ⓐ Ⓑ Ⓒ Ⓓ **8.** "I had twenty dollars, but I bought a pack of gum. I need to remember to do this from my total savings when I get home," said Janice.
   A) subtract   **B)** reconstruct   **C)** attract   **D)** abstract

Ⓐ Ⓑ Ⓒ Ⓓ **9.** Although gophers are very cute, they can create this in a yard due to the many holes they dig under the ground.
   A) destruction   **B)** construction   **C)** distracting   **D)** attractive

Ⓐ Ⓑ Ⓒ Ⓓ **10.** What does the root **struct** mean?
   A) to cover   **B)** to throw   **C)** build   **D)** pull

Ⓐ Ⓑ Ⓒ Ⓓ **11.** What does the root **tract** mean?
   A) to cover   **B)** to throw   **C)** build   **D)** pull

Ⓐ Ⓑ Ⓒ Ⓓ ***12.** What does **sub** mean in the word *substructure*?
   A) over   **B)** under   **C)** more   **D)** cutting

Ⓐ Ⓑ Ⓒ Ⓓ ***13.** What does **super** mean in the word *superstructure*?
   A) over   **B)** under   **C)** after   **D)** better

Ⓐ Ⓑ Ⓒ Ⓓ ***14.** What does **de** most likely mean in the word *destruction*?
   A) down   **B)** up   **C)** path   **D)** build

Ⓐ Ⓑ Ⓒ Ⓓ **15.** Finish this analogy: construct : _____ : : _____ : reconnect
   A) reconstruct : reconnect   **B)** connect : construct
   C) connect : reconnect   **D)** reconstruct : connect

Greek and Latin Roots © 2004 Creative Teaching Press

Word List: therm = heat, temperature

Vocabulary	Definitions
endothermic (adj)	**heated** from within the body
exothermic (adj)	requires **heat** to be absorbed from outside of the body
therm (n)	a unit of **heat** equal to 1,000 great calories
thermal (adj)	related to **heat** or **temperature**
thermodynamic (adj)	caused or operated by **heat** that has changed into different forms of energy
thermograph (n)	a device that automatically writes down (records) changes in **temperature**
thermometer (n)	an instrument that measures **temperature** or **heat**
thermophile (n)	an organism that has adapted to living in very high **temperatures (heat),** such as bacteria or algae
thermos (n)	a container that is used to keep things **warm,** such as your soup; a double-walled container that keeps things **warm**
thermostat (n)	a device used to control the **temperature**

Vocabulary Sort: therm

thermostat	**heated** from within the body
exothermic	a container that is used to keep things **warm,** such as your soup; a double-walled container that keeps things **warm**
thermos	a device that automatically writes down (records) changes in **temperature**
thermograph	a unit of **heat** equal to 1,000 great calories
thermophile	caused or operated by **heat** that has changed into different forms of energy
therm	a device used to control the **temperature**
thermodynamic	an organism that has adapted to living in very high **temperatures (heat),** such as bacteria or algae
endothermic	related to **heat** or **temperature**
thermal	an instrument that measures **temperature** or **heat**
thermometer	requires **heat** to be absorbed from outside of the body

Greek and Latin Roots © 2004 Creative Teaching Press

Read-Around Review: therm

I have the first card.
Who has the root that means **heat** or **temperature?**

I have the root **therm.**
Who has the word that is used to describe something that needs to be around a warm environment to survive since it must be **heated** from outside of its body?

I have the word **exothermic.**
Who has the word that is used to describe anything that is related to **heat** or **temperature?**

I have the word **thermal.**
Who has the word that names something that is possibly in your lunchbox that is insulated to keep food or drinks, such as soup or hot chocolate, warm on a cold day?

I have the word **thermos.**
Who has the word that describes a type of energy that is caused or operated by **heat** that changes forms?

I have the word **thermodynamic.**
Who has the word that names a measurement that is equal to 1,000 great calories ?

I have the word **therm.**
Who has the word that names a device that automatically writes down changes in **temperature?**

I have the word **thermograph.**
Who has the word that names an organism that loves very high **temperatures?**

I have the word **thermophile.**
Who has the word that describes an animal that can warm itself from within its body?

I have the word **endothermic.**
Who has the word that names the instrument used by parents and doctors to figure out if you have a fever since it shows changes in temperature or body **heat?**

I have the word **thermometer.**
Who has the word that names the device in a home or classroom that helps you adjust the **temperature** so that it is not too hot or too cold?

I have the word **thermostat.**
Who has the first card?

Greek and Latin Roots © 2004 Creative Teaching Press

Vocabulary Quiz: therm

Shade in the bubble for the correct word.

Ⓐ Ⓑ Ⓒ Ⓓ   **1.** Most reptiles need to be kept on heat rocks. Therefore, what are they?
A) exothermic   **B)** endothermic   **C)** thermodynamic   **D)** thermos

Ⓐ Ⓑ Ⓒ Ⓓ   **2.** Scientists measure heat in these units of measurement.
A) thermos   **B)** thermals   **C)** thermostats   **D)** therms

Ⓐ Ⓑ Ⓒ Ⓓ   **3.** Having one of these is useful on a long road trip if it is very cold and you want to drink some hot chocolate.
A) thermostat   **B)** thermometer   **C)** thermograph   **D)** thermos

Ⓐ Ⓑ Ⓒ Ⓓ   **4.** If this is broken, then your home will usually be very cold or very hot.
A) thermometer   **B)** thermos   **C)** thermostat   **D)** thermodynamic

Ⓐ Ⓑ Ⓒ Ⓓ   **5.** Living things that can keep themselves warm from within their bodies are described as being which of the following?
A) endothermic   **B)** exothermic   **C)** thermodynamic   **D)** thermal

Ⓐ Ⓑ Ⓒ Ⓓ   **6.** Which word describes a type of blanket that keeps people very warm?
A) thermostatic   **B)** thermal   **C)** thermographic   **D)** thermophile

Ⓐ Ⓑ Ⓒ Ⓓ   **7.** Some scientists keep track of temperature changes by studying the recordings on which machine?
A) thermograph   **B)** thermostat   **C)** thermometer   **D)** thermos

Ⓐ Ⓑ Ⓒ Ⓓ   **8.** The nurse checked Brittany's temperature with this instrument.
A) thermometer   **B)** thermos   **C)** therm   **D)** thermostat

Ⓐ Ⓑ Ⓒ Ⓓ   **9.** You will find many of these in hot, humid places where there is moisture and heat most of the time.
A) thermophiles   **B)** exothermics   **C)** thermostats   **D)** therms

Ⓐ Ⓑ Ⓒ Ⓓ   **10.** Things that work because of energy created by heat are described as being which of the following?
A) thermonuclear   **B)** thermodynamic   **C)** thermal   **D)** therms

Write the correct word on the line so the sentence makes sense.

11. When measuring heat, a change of 3,000 calories could also be described as a change of three _____.

12. You will rarely find _____ animals roaming around the Arctic Circle with bare skin.

13. "Ms. Graves, can we please turn up the heat on the _____? It's cold in here!"

14. The commercial said that the new _____ could keep soup warm for 12 hours!

15. Bacteria are an example of _____, since they grow in heat.

Greek and Latin Roots © 2004 Creative Teaching Press

Word List: socio = companion, friend

Vocabulary	Definitions
antisocial (adj)	against the basic rules of a **group;** harmful to the people in a **group**
associate (n)	a fellow worker or **friend** (usually related to an office)
association (n)	a **group** of people who have gathered based on similar goals or beliefs
disassociate (v)	to break ties with a **group;** to end a **friendship;** to sever a relationship
social (adj)	**friendly;** a person who enjoys **companions**
socialite (n)	a person who is important or of high rank within a specific, usually fashionable **group**
sociogram (n)	a diagram that represents each person's **friends** in a classroom
sociology (n)	the study of how **people** get along
sociopath (n)	a person who suffers from an antisocial mental disorder
unsocial (adj)	not social; having or showing a dislike for others in a **group**

Greek and Latin Roots © 2004 Creative Teaching Press

Vocabulary Sort: socio

sociogram	**friendly;** a person who enjoys **companions**
socialite	a **group** of people who have gathered based on similar goals or beliefs
association	the study of how **people** get along
unsocial	not social; having or showing a dislike for others in a **group**
associate	against the basic rules of a **group;** harmful to the people in a **group**
sociology	a fellow worker or **friend** (usually related to an office)
sociopath	a person who is important or of high rank within a specific, usually fashionable **group**
disassociate	to break ties with a **group;** to end a **friendship;** to sever a relationship
antisocial	a diagram that represents each person's **friends** in a classroom
social	a person who suffers from an antisocial mental disorder

Greek and Latin Roots © 2004 Creative Teaching Press

Read-Around Review: socio

I have the first card.
Who has the root that means **friend** or **companion**?

I have the root **socio.**
Who has the word that names a **group** of people who have gathered together because they share the same goals?

I have the word **association.**
Who has the word that names a diagram that represents each person's **friends** in a classroom?

I have the word **sociogram.**
Who has the word that identifies an area of study that focuses on how people get along?

I have the word **sociology.**
Who has the word that describes a person who is simply **friendly?**

I have the word **social.**
Who has the word that names a person who is thought to be very important within a **group?**

I have the word **socialite.**
Who has the word that names a person who suffers from an antisocial mental disorder?

I have the word **sociopath.**
Who has the word that names a fellow worker?

I have the word **associate.**
Who has the word that describes a person who does not like being around other people?

I have the word **unsocial.**
Who has the word that describes what a person does when he leaves a **group** and decides not to be a part of it anymore?

I have the word **disassociate.**
Who has the word that describes a person who goes against the rules of the **group?**

I have the word **antisocial.**
Who has the first card?

Greek and Latin Roots © 2004 Creative Teaching Press

Name _____ Date _____

Vocabulary Quiz: socio

Shade in the bubble for the correct word.

Ⓐ Ⓑ Ⓒ Ⓓ   **1.** What is the adjective used to describe a person who is friendly?
          A) sociopath   **B)** socialite   **C)** associate   **D)** social

Ⓐ Ⓑ Ⓒ Ⓓ   **2.** What class could you take in college if you are interested in learning about how people get along with each other?
          A) sociology   **B)** antisocial   **C)** sociogram   **D)** association

Ⓐ Ⓑ Ⓒ Ⓓ   **3.** What do you call someone who keeps to himself and doesn't have any interest in being a part of a group?
          A) socialite   **B)** unsocial   **C)** sociopath   **D)** associate

Ⓐ Ⓑ Ⓒ Ⓓ   **4.** What is the name of a group that has formed for a common goal?
          A) association   **B)** sociopath   **C)** associate   **D)** sociology

Ⓐ Ⓑ Ⓒ Ⓓ   **5.** A person who has a mental condition that causes him to act out in bad ways toward society is called a(n) _____.
          A) sociopath   **B)** antisocial   **C)** socialite   **D)** associate

Ⓐ Ⓑ Ⓒ Ⓓ   **6.** If you decide to spend time with new friends without spending time with your old friends, what did you do to your old friends?
          A) associate   **B)** disassociate   **C)** socialize   **D)** antisocial

Ⓐ Ⓑ Ⓒ Ⓓ   **7.** In Room 2b, Mrs. Arias made a diagram matching each student with his or her friends. What type of diagram did she make?
          A) disassociation   **B)** sociopath   **C)** socialite   **D)** sociogram

Ⓐ Ⓑ Ⓒ Ⓓ   **8.** A socially prominent person is known as this.
          A) socialite   **B)** sociogram   **C)** sociopath   **D)** associate

Ⓐ Ⓑ Ⓒ Ⓓ   **9.** The man on the news was arrested because he was showing behavior that broke the rules of society. What was his behavior?
          A) socialite   **B)** associative   **C)** antisocial   **D)** social

Ⓐ Ⓑ Ⓒ Ⓓ   **10.** The law firm has hired two new people to work in the office. What are they called?
          A) sociopaths   **B)** associates   **C)** socialites   **D)** social

Write the correct word on the line so the sentence makes sense.

11. It's always nice to be _____ when being introduced to new people.

12. The National Wildlife _____ is trying to save several endangered species.

13. When someone is mean to you year after year, perhaps it is time to _____ from him.

14. The cameras took many pictures of the _____ as they came out of the limousine.

15. The most popular class at the university was _____, since the students enjoyed learning about how people get along.

Greek and Latin Roots © 2004 Creative Teaching Press

Name _____   Date _____

Review Test: therm and socio

Shade in the bubble for the correct word.

Ⓐ Ⓑ Ⓒ Ⓓ   **1.** What do you call an animal that keeps itself warm from within its own body?
A) exothermic   **B)** endothermic   **C)** sociable   **D)** thermostatic

Ⓐ Ⓑ Ⓒ Ⓓ   **2.** When you are a member of this, you must follow the rules.
A) society   **B)** thermometer   **C)** antisocial   **D)** sociology

Ⓐ Ⓑ Ⓒ Ⓓ   **3.** "Please move it down. It's too hot in here," said Mr. Frederick. What did he want changed?
A) sociopaths   **B)** thermometer   **C)** thermostat   **D)** thermals

Ⓐ Ⓑ Ⓒ Ⓓ   **4.** Chelsea is very friendly toward others. What is she considered to be?
A) sociopath   **B)** thermodynamic   **C)** unsocial   **D)** social

Ⓐ Ⓑ Ⓒ Ⓓ   **5.** When you quit a club or a group because you don't want to be around the people anymore, what do you do to them?
A) associate   **B)** disassociate   **C)** therm   **D)** sociopath

Ⓐ Ⓑ Ⓒ Ⓓ   **6.** What popular class teaches students about how people in a group get along?
A) sociology   **B)** thermodynamics   **C)** endothermic   **D)** society

Ⓐ Ⓑ Ⓒ Ⓓ   **7.** What does the law call a person with an antisocial mental disorder who may harm others?
A) sociopath   **B)** socialite   **C)** antisocial   **D)** unsocial

Ⓐ Ⓑ Ⓒ Ⓓ   **8.** What is used to figure out whether or not you have a fever?
A) thermostat   **B)** thermos   **C)** thermometer   **D)** sociopath

Ⓐ Ⓑ Ⓒ Ⓓ   **9.** If you prefer to spend time by yourself instead of joining a group, you may be acting a bit like this.
A) sociable   **B)** thermal   **C)** unsocial   **D)** associated

Ⓐ Ⓑ Ⓒ Ⓓ   **10.** What does the root **socio** mean?
A) friend   **B)** apart from   **C)** to cut   **D)** heat

Ⓐ Ⓑ Ⓒ Ⓓ   **11.** What does the root **therm** mean?
A) friendly   **B)** apart from   **C)** to cut   **D)** heat

Ⓐ Ⓑ Ⓒ Ⓓ   ***12.** What does **dis** mean in the word *disassociate*?
A) together   **B)** not   **C)** friendly   **D)** a group

Ⓐ Ⓑ Ⓒ Ⓓ   ***13.** What does **graph** mean in the word *thermograph*?
A) writing   **B)** holding   **C)** friendly   **D)** heated

Ⓐ Ⓑ Ⓒ Ⓓ   ***14.** What does **exo** most likely mean in the word *exothermic*?
A) heat   **B)** life   **C)** inside   **D)** outside

Ⓐ Ⓑ Ⓒ Ⓓ   **15.** If you disassociate from a group, what do you do?
A) join in   **B)** quit   **C)** bring snacks   **D)** get bored

Greek and Latin Roots © 2004 Creative Teaching Press

Word List: phon, phono, phone = sound, voice

Vocabulary	Definitions
cacophony (n)	harsh **sounds;** bad noise
dysphonia (n)	difficulty producing speech **sounds,** usually due to hoarseness
euphonic (adj)	having a nice **sound;** pleasant combination of sounds in words
gramophone (n)	a device used to play the **sounds** of music as written on records
homophone (n)	a word that has the same **sound** but a different meaning as another word
megaphone (n)	a large funnel-shaped device used to make the **voice sound** louder by directing the **sound** waves straight out to listeners (most often used by cheer teams)
microphone (n)	a device used to make small **voices sound** larger, especially in a big room
phonics (n)	the **sounds** that letters make and the letters that are used to represent **sounds**
phonology (n)	the study of speech **sounds** in language
saxophone (n)	a woodwind instrument that sends out **sounds** through its curved, metal body.

Greek and Latin Roots © 2004 Creative Teaching Press

Vocabulary Sort: phon, phono, phone

homophone	a device used to make small **voices sound** larger, especially in a big room
phonology	a woodwind instrument that sends out **sounds** through its curved, metal body
euphonic	a device used to play the **sounds** of music as written on records
megaphone	harsh **sounds;** bad noise
dysphonia	the study of speech **sounds**
saxophone	a large funnel-shaped device used to make the **voice sound** louder by directing the **sound** waves straight out to listeners (most often used by cheer teams)
cacophony	difficulty producing speech **sounds,** usually due to hoarseness
gramophone	having a nice **sound;** pleasant combination of **sounds** in words
microphone	the **sounds** that letters make and the letters that are used to represent **sounds**
phonics	a word that has the same **sound** but a different meaning as another word

Greek and Latin Roots © 2004 Creative Teaching Press

Read-Around Review: phon, phono, phone

I have the first card.
Who has the roots that mean **sound** or **voice?**

I have the roots **phon, phono,** and **phone.**
Who has the word that identifies what you would be playing in the orchestra if it was a woodwind instrument that sent **sounds** out of its curved body?

I have the word **saxophone.**
Who has the word that names the device used to make small **sounds** louder?

I have the word **microphone.**
Who has the word that names words that have the same **sound** but different meanings?

I have the word **homophones.**
Who has the word that names what you hear if there are harsh **sounds** that hurt your ears?

I have the word **cacophony.**
Who has the word that names what you learn in the early grades to help you read since it involves matching letters to **sounds?**

I have the word **phonics.**
Who has the word that names a large funnel-shaped device that some people use instead of yelling in a stadium so they can send their **voices** out farther to more people?

I have the word **megaphone.**
Who has the word that identifies the study of speech **sounds?**

I have the word **phonology.**
Who has the word that names a condition in which a person has temporary problems making speech **sounds?**

I have the word **dysphonia.**
Who has the word that names the machine that played old records when you turned a lever?

I have the word **gramophone.**
Who has the word that describes a nice sound that is pleasing to your ears?

I have the word **euphonic.**
Who has the first card?

Greek and Latin Roots © 2004 Creative Teaching Press

Name _____ Date _____

Vocabulary Quiz: phon, phono, phone

Shade in the bubble for the correct word.

Ⓐ Ⓑ Ⓒ Ⓓ   **1.** What would you see cheerleaders using at a football game in high school?
     A) megaphones   **B)** saxophones   **C)** gramophones   **D)** phonics

Ⓐ Ⓑ Ⓒ Ⓓ   **2.** What skill are you using when you read words by matching sounds to the letters?
     A) phonology   **B)** phonics   **C)** dysphonia   **D)** cacophony

Ⓐ Ⓑ Ⓒ Ⓓ   **3.** If you hear a terrible sound and you immediately want to plug your ears, what are you hearing?
     A) cacophony   **B)** euphonic   **C)** phonology   **D)** gramophones

Ⓐ Ⓑ Ⓒ Ⓓ   **4.** What do we call two words that sound the same but have different meanings?
     A) gramophones   **B)** phonics   **C)** saxophones   **D)** homophones

Ⓐ Ⓑ Ⓒ Ⓓ   **5.** Which word names an invention that made music come out of a machine?
     A) microphone   **B)** phonology   **C)** megaphone   **D)** gramophone

Ⓐ Ⓑ Ⓒ Ⓓ   **6.** If you like what you hear, which adjective might you use to describe the sound?
     A) dysphonic   **B)** cacophonic   **C)** phonics   **D)** euphonic

Ⓐ Ⓑ Ⓒ Ⓓ   **7.** What is commonly used to make voices sound louder in large rooms?
     A) saxophone   **B)** microphone   **C)** gramophone   **D)** phonology

Ⓐ Ⓑ Ⓒ Ⓓ   **8.** The study of speech sounds is called _____.
     A) phonics   **B)** euphonic   **C)** phonology   **D)** cacophony

Ⓐ Ⓑ Ⓒ Ⓓ   **9.** Every once in a while, a famous singer will have to cancel a concert due to which problem?
     A) cacophony   **B)** euphonic   **C)** phonology   **D)** dysphonia

Ⓐ Ⓑ Ⓒ Ⓓ   **10.** Which woodwind instrument sends sounds out of its curved body?
     A) saxophone   **B)** megaphone   **C)** microphone   **D)** gramophone

Write the correct word on the line so the sentence makes sense.

11. The first day of band rehearsal made the band leader think that all the students' instruments sounded like a _____ because of all the squeaks he heard.

12. When you look at a letter and make the sound, you are practicing _____.

13. Many famous orchestras may be described as _____.

14. "We can't hear you back here. Please use the _____."

15. A _____ would be considered an antique and would probably be worth some money if it could still produce correct sounds.

Greek and Latin Roots © 2004 Creative Teaching Press

Word List: strain, strict, string = bind, tie, or draw tight

Vocabulary	Definitions
astringent (n)	a substance used on skin to make the skin **tight**
boa constrictor (n)	a snake that kills its prey by squeezing it **tightly**
constrict (v)	to hold in; to make smaller; to squeeze or **bind** to make smaller
district (n)	a region or area that is **bound** together by specific rules, laws, resources, and/or money
restrain (v)	to hold back; to keep under control; to limit; to **draw tight** by force
restricted (adj)	**bound** by limits; kept within certain rules
strain (v)	to draw or stretch **tight** beyond the normal limits
strainer (n)	a device used for letting the water leave the food so the food is **drawn** together
string (n)	a thin piece of twisted fiber that can be used to **tie** things together
stringent (adj)	demanding strict attention to rules; rigid; having a **tight** set of rules

Greek and Latin Roots © 2004 Creative Teaching Press

Vocabulary Sort: strain, strict, string

strainer	**bound** by limits; kept within certain rules
restrain	a region or area that is **bound** together by specific rules, laws, resources, and/or money
boa constrictor	a substance used on skin to make the skin **tight**
string	to hold back; to keep under control; to limit; to **draw tight** by force
strain	demanding strict attention to rules; rigid; having a **tight** set of rules
astringent	a device used for letting the water leave the food so the food is **drawn** together
stringent	a snake that kills its prey by squeezing it **tightly**
constrict	to draw or stretch **tight** beyond the normal limits
district	to hold in; to make smaller; to squeeze or **bind** to make smaller
restricted	a thin piece of twisted fiber that can be used to **tie** things together

Greek and Latin Roots © 2004 Creative Teaching Press

Read-Around Review: strain, strict, string

I have the first card.
Who has the roots that mean **bind, tie,** or **draw tight?**

I have the roots **strain, strict,** and **string.**
Who has the word that describes what you do to your muscles if you pull them too **tightly?**

I have the word **strain.**
Who has the word that identifies a snake that kills its prey by squeezing it **tightly?**

I have the word **boa constrictor.**
Who has the word that identifies what children are put on to make them follow **tighter** rules when they misbehave?

I have the word **restriction.**
Who has the word that names the kitchen tool often used to get water out of pasta noodles?

I have the word **strainer.**
Who has the word that means demanding strict attention to rules?

I have the word **stringent.**
Who has the word that names a liquid usually put on the face to make the skin **tighter** to keep out the dirt and oil?

I have the word **astringent.**
Who has the word that names an area that has its own rules and goals?

I have the word **district.**
Who has the word that names a thin piece of any kind of material that can **tie** things together?

I have the word **string.**
Who has the word that describes what someone does when she makes something smaller by squeezing it?

I have the word **constrict.**
Who has the word that describes what someone has to do to hold an animal back when it is upset?

I have the word **restrain.**
Who has the first card?

Greek and Latin Roots © 2004 Creative Teaching Press

Name _____   Date _____

Vocabulary Quiz: strain, strict, string

Shade in the bubble for the correct word.

Ⓐ Ⓑ Ⓒ Ⓓ **1.** Lisa watched television instead of doing her homework. She will most likely not be allowed to watch any more television. What is another word for this?
A) district   B) constrict   C) strainer   D) restricted

Ⓐ Ⓑ Ⓒ Ⓓ **2.** Which type of snake squeezes its prey?
A) raptor   B) boa constrictor   C) viper   D) rattlesnake

Ⓐ Ⓑ Ⓒ Ⓓ **3.** If you do this to a muscle, then you might walk with a limp for a while.
A) stringent   B) constrict   C) restrain   D) strain

Ⓐ Ⓑ Ⓒ Ⓓ **4.** What can be used to wrap newspapers into a bundle for recycling?
A) strain   B) astringent   C) strainer   D) string

Ⓐ Ⓑ Ⓒ Ⓓ **5.** What is another word that describes a rigid and strict set of rules?
A) strain   B) stringent   C) district   D) restrain

Ⓐ Ⓑ Ⓒ Ⓓ **6.** "Mom, where's that kitchen gadget that drains the water out?" asked Julie. What was Julie looking for?
A) strain   B) restrictor   C) boa constrictor D) strainer

Ⓐ Ⓑ Ⓒ Ⓓ **7.** Many years ago, women wore tight garments called corsets that squeezed their upper bodies to make them look smaller. What did the corsets do?
A) constricted   B) restricted   C) strained   D) districted

Ⓐ Ⓑ Ⓒ Ⓓ **8.** What is a section of a state that forms its own rules and goals called?
A) district   B) constrictor   C) astringent   D) restraining

Ⓐ Ⓑ Ⓒ Ⓓ **9.** Some people like to put this on their face because it makes their face feel clean and fresh.
A) restraint   B) boa constrictors C) astringent   D) strainers

Ⓐ Ⓑ Ⓒ Ⓓ **10.** In the movie, the police officer had to do this to the car thief until back-up help arrived.
A) constrict   B) restrain   C) restrict   D) district

Write the correct word on the line so the sentence makes sense.

11. "If you don't take the trash out right now, then you'll be _____ from going to the game," said Dad.

12. The girls like to tie the _____ together and use it to play a game.

13. Each _____ has a set of rules that must be followed.

14. It's always smart to stretch before exercising in order to prevent a _____ on the muscles.

15. "Wow! This _____ makes my face smell like lemons!" said Juan.

Greek and Latin Roots © 2004 Creative Teaching Press

Name _____   Date _____

Review Test: phon, phone, phono and strain, strict, string

Shade in the bubble for the correct word.

Ⓐ Ⓑ Ⓒ Ⓓ   **1.** What liquid do people often put on their face to draw it tighter and make it feel more refreshed?
   A) strainer   **B)** dysphonia   **C)** restraint   **D)** astringent

Ⓐ Ⓑ Ⓒ Ⓓ   **2.** How does a boa constrictor kill its prey so it can survive?
   A) venom   **B)** bites it   **C)** squeezes it   **D)** stomps on it

Ⓐ Ⓑ Ⓒ Ⓓ   **3.** If you hear music or poetry that you think is beautiful, you might use this word when telling someone else about it.
   A) cacophony   **B)** euphonic   **C)** phonics   **D)** restriction

Ⓐ Ⓑ Ⓒ Ⓓ   **4.** What do we call words that sound the same but have different meanings?
   A) homophones   **B)** phonics   **C)** euphonics   **D)** gramophones

Ⓐ Ⓑ Ⓒ Ⓓ   **5.** Mr. David studies speech sounds. What is his job title on his business card?
   A) gramophone   **B)** phonologist   **C)** strainer   **D)** saxophonist

Ⓐ Ⓑ Ⓒ Ⓓ   **6.** What is the name of the kitchen tool used for getting the water out of foods such as spaghetti?
   A) strainer   **B)** constrictor   **C)** cacophony   **D)** stringent

Ⓐ Ⓑ Ⓒ Ⓓ   **7.** What is the name of the punishment that usually binds someone to tighter rules, less fun, and tighter limits?
   A) restraining   **B)** phonics   **C)** district   **D)** restriction

Ⓐ Ⓑ Ⓒ Ⓓ   **8.** A wild dog about to attack will need someone to quickly do this to it.
   A) restrain   **B)** strain   **C)** phonology   **D)** stringent

Ⓐ Ⓑ Ⓒ Ⓓ   **9.** Terrible noises that drive a person crazy could be called this.
   A) euphonia   **B)** phonology   **C)** microphone   **D)** cacophony

Ⓐ Ⓑ Ⓒ Ⓓ   **10.** What does the root **phon** mean?
   A) sound   **B)** to listen   **C)** to cut   **D)** to make tighter

Ⓐ Ⓑ Ⓒ Ⓓ   **11.** What do the roots **strain, strict,** and **string** mean?
   A) sound   **B)** to listen   **C)** to cut   **D)** to make tighter

Ⓐ Ⓑ Ⓒ Ⓓ   *****12.** What does **ology** mean in the word *phonology*?
   A) person who   **B)** able to do   **C)** study of   **D)** sound

Ⓐ Ⓑ Ⓒ Ⓓ   *****13.** What does **mega** mean in the word *megaphone*?
   A) large   **B)** small   **C)** sound   **D)** tighter

Ⓐ Ⓑ Ⓒ Ⓓ   *****14.** What does **eu** most likely mean in the word *euphonic*?
   A) sound   **B)** choir   **C)** bad   **D)** good

Ⓐ Ⓑ Ⓒ Ⓓ   *****15.** What does **micro** most likely mean in the word *microphone*?
   A) large   **B)** small   **C)** bad   **D)** good

Greek and Latin Roots © 2004 Creative Teaching Press

Word List: terr, terra, geo = land; earth

Vocabulary	Definitions
extraterrestrial (adj)	out of this world; above and beyond what is found on planet **Earth**
geode (n)	a hollow stone found on the **earth** that is lined on the inside with crystals
geographer (n)	a person who studies the regions of the **earth,** including the climates and natural resources
geography (n)	the science of the **earth** that deals with the regions or places on the planet's surface
geology (n)	the study of the **earth,** specifically rocks and the planet's crust
mediterranean (adj)	almost or completely surrounded by **land**
subterranean (adj)	under the surface of the **earth;** underground
terra cotta (n)	baked **earth;** hard, brownish-red pottery
terrace (n)	a raised, flat mound of **earth** (dirt) that looks like a platform with sloping sides
territory (n)	an area, region, or piece of **land**

Vocabulary Sort: terr, terra, geo

geology	an area, region, or piece of **land**
mediterranean	under the surface of the **earth;** underground
territory	a person who studies the regions of the **earth,** including the climates and natural resources
extraterrestrial	the science of the **earth** that deals with the regions or places on the planet's surface
geode	baked **earth;** hard, brownish-red pottery
geography	almost or completely surrounded by **land**
terra cotta	a raised, flat mound of **earth** (dirt) that looks like a platform with sloping sides
terrace	out of this world; above and beyond what is found on planet **Earth**
geographer	a hollow stone found on the **earth** that is lined on the inside with crystals
subterranean	the study of the **earth,** specifically rocks and the planet's crust

Greek and Latin Roots © 2004 Creative Teaching Press

Read-Around Review: terr, terra, geo

I have the first card.
Who has the roots that mean **earth** or **land?**

I have the roots **terr, terra,** and **geo.**
Who has the word that describes an area that is completely surrounded by **land?**

I have the word **mediterranean.**
Who has the word that names things that are under the **earth?**

I have the word **subterranean.**
Who has the word that identifies a type of pottery that is reddish brown without any glazing?

I have the word **terra cotta.**
Who has the word that names a person who studies the **earth?**

I have the word **geographer.**
Who has the word that names the branch of science that involves studying the **earth,**
particularly the rocks and the **earth's** crust?

I have the word **geology.**
Who has the word that identifies raised, flat mounds of dirt that look like stair steps
made out of soil with sides that slope down?

I have the word **terraces.**
Who has the word that identifies what you would want to study if you are interested in where
things are located on planet **Earth** such as the countries, towns, lakes, and oceans?

I have the word **geography.**
Who has the word that names an area or region of **land?**

I have the word **territory.**
Who has the word that describes anything that is from another planet or literally
"out of this world"?

I have the word **extraterrestrial.**
Who has the word that identifies a particular type of stone that has beautiful crystals
hidden inside of it?

I have the word **geode.**
Who has the first card?

Greek and Latin Roots © 2004 Creative Teaching Press

Name _____ Date _____

Vocabulary Quiz: terr, terra, geo

Shade in the bubble for the correct word.

Ⓐ Ⓑ Ⓒ Ⓓ   **1.** When you watch outer space movies or read books about science fiction, you are sure to hear or read this word.
   A) extraterrestrial   **B)** terrace   **C)** terra cotta   **D)** geode

Ⓐ Ⓑ Ⓒ Ⓓ   **2.** At some home or jewelry shows, you will find these crystals for sale in their natural state.
   A) terra cotta   **B)** terraces   **C)** geographers   **D)** geodes

Ⓐ Ⓑ Ⓒ Ⓓ   **3.** What do you call the study of land and how it is broken up into regions?
   A) geology   **B)** geography   **C)** territory   **D)** terraces

Ⓐ Ⓑ Ⓒ Ⓓ   **4.** An area that is completely surrounded by dry land is called this.
   A) mediterranean   **B)** subterranean   **C)** terrace   **D)** geode

Ⓐ Ⓑ Ⓒ Ⓓ   **5.** Dogs are fond of burying their bones, which are later found in this part of ground.
   A) mediterranean   **B)** terraces   **C)** geodes   **D)** subterranean

Ⓐ Ⓑ Ⓒ Ⓓ   **6.** A piece of land that is named and under particular rule could be called this.
   A) terrace   **B)** territory   **C)** geology   **D)** geode

Ⓐ Ⓑ Ⓒ Ⓓ   **7.** If a piece of pottery came from Mexico, there is a good chance that it is this type.
   A) terra cotta   **B)** terraced   **C)** subterranean   **D)** mediterranean

Ⓐ Ⓑ Ⓒ Ⓓ   **8.** What do we call the study of rocks and the earth's crust?
   A) geography   **B)** paleontology   **C)** geology   **D)** geode

Ⓐ Ⓑ Ⓒ Ⓓ   **9.** What do we call a person who studies where cities, countries, and continents are located?
   A) geologist   **B)** geographer   **C)** geode   **D)** terrace

Ⓐ Ⓑ Ⓒ Ⓓ   **10.** On a cross-country drive, you will most likely see some of these raised, flat mounds of earth.
   A) terra cottas   **B)** geodes   **C)** geographers   **D)** terraces

Write the correct word on the line so the sentence makes sense.

11. If you collect hollow stones lined with crystals, then you collect _____.

12. "Look! This _____ bowl will look perfect in my reddish-brown kitchen!"

13. The _____ was so excited to find the igneous rocks.

14. Do you know where different countries of the world are located? Are you good in _____?

15. Anything related to UFOs would be in the _____ category.

Greek and Latin Roots © 2004 Creative Teaching Press

Word List: naut, naus, nav = relating to the sea, ships, or travelers

Vocabulary	Definitions
Argonaut (n)	a person who took part in the California Gold Rush by **traveling** west in search of gold from 1848–1849
astronaut (n)	a person who is trained to **travel** into outer space
circumnavigate (v)	to **travel** around the earth on water or in the air
cosmonaut (n)	a Soviet who is trained to **travel** into outer space
nauseous (adj)	affected with a feeling of sickness in the stomach that feels like **sea** sickness
nautical (adj)	related to sailing, sailors, or **ships**
navigable (adj)	wide or deep enough for **ships** to be able to pass through
navigate (v)	to steer or direct a **ship** or airplane
navigator (n)	a person who is trained to plan the course of and drive a **ship**
navy (n)	a fleet of **ships;** all the **warships** of a nation

Greek and Latin Roots © 2004 Creative Teaching Press

Vocabulary Sort: naut, naus, nav

astronaut	a feeling of sickness in the stomach that feels like **sea** sickness
nautical	to **travel** around the earth on water or in the air
navy	a person who is trained to plan the course of and drive a **ship**
navigator	to steer or direct a **ship** or airplane
Argonaut	a Soviet who is trained to **travel** into outer space
nauseous	wide or deep enough for **ships** to be able to pass through
cosmonaut	a fleet of **ships**; all the **warships** of a nation
navigate	a person who took part in the California Gold Rush by **traveling** west in search of gold from 1848–1849
navigable	related to sailing, sailors, or **ships**
circumnavigate	a person who is trained to **travel** into outer space

Greek and Latin Roots © 2004 Creative Teaching Press

Read-Around Review: naut, naus, nav

I have the first card.
Who has the roots that mean **sea, ships,** or **travelers?**

I have the roots **naut, naus,** and **nav.**
Who has the word that describes a passageway that is not blocked and is deep enough
for **ships** to go through?

I have the word **navigable.**
Who has the word that describes how some people feel when a **ship** or boat rocks too much?

I have the word **nauseous.**
Who has the word that names a Soviet who was trained to go into outer space?

I have the word **cosmonaut.**
Who has the word that identifies a person who participated in the California Gold Rush?

I have the word **Argonaut.**
Who has the word that tells what the captain of a ship does as he steers his **ship?**

I have the word **navigates.**
Who has the word that describes anything that is related to sailing, sailors, or **ships?**

I have the word **nautical.**
Who has the word that describes what a captain may do if he decides to steer his
ship around the continent of Australia?

I have the word **circumnavigate.**
Who has the word that names a fleet of **ships** that help protect a country?

I have the word **navy.**
Who has the word that names the person in charge of planning the course of the **ship?**

I have the word **navigator.**
Who has the word that identifies a person who is trained in the United States to **travel** into
outer space in a space shuttle?

I have the word **astronaut.**
Who has the first card?

Greek and Latin Roots © 2004 Creative Teaching Press

Name _____   Date _____

Vocabulary Quiz: naut, naus, nav

Shade in the bubble for the correct word.

Ⓐ Ⓑ Ⓒ Ⓓ   **1.** Most countries that are near an ocean have one of these military units to help protect their land. What is it called?
   A) nautical   **B)** cosmonaut   **C)** navigator   **D)** navy

Ⓐ Ⓑ Ⓒ Ⓓ   **2.** If you ever decide to take a worldwide cruise for a year, you will be able to do this to the globe.
   A) circumnavigate   **B)** astronaut   **C)** navigable   **D)** navigate

Ⓐ Ⓑ Ⓒ Ⓓ   **3.** This is a popular goal for many children to become when they dream of going into outer space to investigate the solar system. What do many American children want to become?
   A) astronauts   **B)** cosmonauts   **C)** nauseous   **D)** Argonauts

Ⓐ Ⓑ Ⓒ Ⓓ   **4.** Much of the Arctic Ocean would not be described as this due to the many glaciers and icebergs along the way.
   A) circumnavigated   **B)** nauseous   **C)** in the navy   **D)** navigable

Ⓐ Ⓑ Ⓒ Ⓓ   **5.** If your dream is to someday drive the ship as a captain, what will you need to learn how to do?
   A) cosmonaut   **B)** be an Argonaut   **C)** navigate   **D)** nauseous

Ⓐ Ⓑ Ⓒ Ⓓ   **6.** Miles are measured on the sea as well as on land; however, the length is different. Which word do you think goes before the word "mile" when measuring distance over the oceans?
   A) nauseous   **B)** navigator   **C)** astronaut   **D)** nautical

Ⓐ Ⓑ Ⓒ Ⓓ   **7.** People who easily feel like this usually stay far away from boats and ships.
   A) nautical   **B)** cosmonautical   **C)** navigational   **D)** nauseous

Ⓐ Ⓑ Ⓒ Ⓓ   **8.** You can study about these important travelers by researching the Gold Rush.
   A) Argonauts   **B)** cosmonauts   **C)** astronauts   **D)** navigators

Ⓐ Ⓑ Ⓒ Ⓓ   **9.** Did you know that these people actually beat the Americans to the moon?
   A) Argonauts   **B)** astronauts   **C)** cosmonauts   **D)** navigators

Ⓐ Ⓑ Ⓒ Ⓓ   **10.** Who plans where the ship will travel and what stops will be made along the way?
   A) navigator   **B)** nauseous driver   **C)** Argonaut   **D)** cosmonaut

Write the correct word on the line so the sentence makes sense.

11. The ship's _____ planned three stops for the six-day cruise around Hawaii.

12. Many kids in the United States dream of one day becoming _____ so they can travel to outer space.

13. She designed her bedroom with a _____ theme, with boats and pictures of famous sailors everywhere.

14. I need to lie down. I'm feeling a bit _____.

15. Finish this analogy: _____ : Russia :: _____ : America

Greek and Latin Roots © 2004 Creative Teaching Press

Review Test: terr, terra, geo and naus, naut, nav

Shade in the bubble for the correct word.

Ⓐ Ⓑ Ⓒ Ⓓ   **1.** Some people enjoy collecting these because they admire the beautiful crystals inside.
A) geography   **B)** terraces   **C)** cosmonauts   **D)** geodes

Ⓐ Ⓑ Ⓒ Ⓓ   **2.** Anything that is out of this world is said to be this.
A) extraterrestrial   **B)** geological   **C)** mediterranean   **D)** subterranean

Ⓐ Ⓑ Ⓒ Ⓓ   **3.** These heroes risked their lives so that we would know more about the moon and our solar system.
A) astronauts   **B)** geologists   **C)** geographers   **D)** navigators

Ⓐ Ⓑ Ⓒ Ⓓ   **4.** What is the branch of the military that includes warships and sailors who are trained to protect land and sea?
A) navigator   **B)** extraterrestrial   **C)** geographer   **D)** navy

Ⓐ Ⓑ Ⓒ Ⓓ   **5.** What type of pottery is brownish-red and looks like it came straight from the earth?
A) territory   **B)** terrace   **C)** nauseous   **D)** terra cotta

Ⓐ Ⓑ Ⓒ Ⓓ   **6.** Anything that comes from under the ground or lives under the ground is described as this.
A) mediterranean   **B)** extraterrestrial   **C)** subterranean   **D)** nautical

Ⓐ Ⓑ Ⓒ Ⓓ   **7.** If a sailor travels around the world, he will do what to the globe?
A) navigate   **B)** circumnavigate   **C)** geology   **D)** terrace

Ⓐ Ⓑ Ⓒ Ⓓ   **8.** Who is the person who studies where regions are located on earth?
A) geographer   **B)** geologist   **C)** extraterrestrial   **D)** navigator

Ⓐ Ⓑ Ⓒ Ⓓ   **9.** What do we call a specific area or piece of land?
A) terra cotta   **B)** terrace   **C)** geology   **D)** territory

Ⓐ Ⓑ Ⓒ Ⓓ   **10.** What does the root **terr** mean?
A) sea   **B)** land   **C)** air   **D)** space

Ⓐ Ⓑ Ⓒ Ⓓ   **11.** What do the roots **naus, naut,** and **nav** mean?
A) sea   **B)** land   **C)** air   **D)** space

Ⓐ Ⓑ Ⓒ Ⓓ   ***12.** What does **sub** mean in the word *subterranean*?
A) under   **B)** over   **C)** earth   **D)** water

Ⓐ Ⓑ Ⓒ Ⓓ   ***13.** What does **extra** mean in the word *extraterrestrial*?
A) out of   **B)** better   **C)** earth   **D)** water

Ⓐ Ⓑ Ⓒ Ⓓ   **14.** Finish this analogy: geologist : _____ :: biologist : _____
A) water, land   **B)** life, rocks   **C)** water, rocks   **D)** rocks, life

Ⓐ Ⓑ Ⓒ Ⓓ   **15.** Finish this analogy: _____ : space :: navigator : _____
A) outer, sea   **B)** astronaut, sea   **C)** sea, astronaut   **D)** aviator, navy

Greek and Latin Roots © 2004 Creative Teaching Press

Answer Key

Page 10	Page 19	Page 28	Page 37	Page 46
1. a	1. b	1. b	1. d	1. b
2. b	2. a	2. b	2. b	2. c
3. d	3. d	3. d	3. a	3. c
4. a	4. d	4. d	4. b	4. b
5. d	5. d	5. a	5. b	5. d
6. c	6. c	6. a	6. a	6. a
7. b	7. a	7. b	7. d	7. d
8. a	8. a	8. c	8. c	8. b
9. a	9. a	9. d	9. b	9. c
10. a	10. a	10. a	10. c	10. a
11. impediment	11. spectacle	11. subject	11. exports	11. autobiographies
12. peddlers	12. retrospective	12. interjection	12. imports	12. autograph
13. pedestrians	13. spectacles	13. projector	13. portable	13. cartography
14. pedicure	14. spectators	14. projectile	14. porter	14. seismograph
15. quadrupeds, bipeds	15. perspective	15. dejected	15. transport	15. biography

Page 14	Page 23	Page 32	Page 41	Page 50
1. a	1. b	1. b	1. d	1. d
2. d	2. c	2. a	2. c	2. b
3. b	3. d	3. a	3. a	3. c
4. a	4. a	4. a	4. b	4. c
5. c	5. a	5. d	5. a	5. b
6. b	6. c	6. c	6. b	6. d
7. b	7. b	7. a	7. c	7. a
8. a	8. a	8. c	8. a	8. a
9. a	9. a	9. b	9. d	9. d
10. b	10. d	10. d	10. a	10. b
11. manicures	11. predict	11. sectional	11. Admit	11. transcribing
12. manipulate	12. dictator	12. intersection	12. remit	12. prescription
13. maneuver	13. indictment	13. bisect	13. emit, emit	13. subscription
14. mandates	14. dictionary	14. sector	14. omit	14. script
15. manager	15. diction	15. bisect, trisect, quadrisect	15. intermission	15. describe

Page 15	Page 24	Page 33	Page 42	Page 51
1. c	1. d	1. d	1. b	1. b
2. b	2. c	2. b	2. b	2. b
3. d	3. b	3. a	3. d	3. d
4. d	4. b	4. a	4. a	4. d
5. a	5. a	5. b	5. b	5. a
6. b	6. d	6. d	6. c	6. a
7. a	7. c	7. b	7. a	7. d
8. b	8. d	8. d	8. c	8. a
9. d	9. a	9. c	9. d	9. a
10. a	10. a	10. c	10. b	10. b
11. b	11. b	11. b	11. a	11. b
12. d	12. d	12. d	12. d	12. a
13. c	13. b	13. a	13. a	13. b
14. c	14. c	14. b	14. b	14. a
15. b	15. b	15. b	15. d	15. a

Answer Key

Page 55	Page 64	Page 73	Page 82	Page 91
1. a	1. d	1. a	1. c	1. a
2. d	2. b	2. d	2. b	2. d
3. a	3. a	3. d	3. a	3. b
4. d	4. d	4. b	4. b	4. b
5. a	5. a	5. c	5. a	5. a
6. b	6. a	6. a	6. d	6. d
7. a	7. a	7. b	7. a	7. a
8. a	8. d	8. a	8. a	8. a
9. b	9. a	9. d	9. a	9. d
10. a	10. a	10. a	10. d	10. c
11. incredulous	11. bonus	11. autobiography	11. reflection	11. conjunction
12. creed	12. beneficial	12. antibiotics	12. inflexible, flexible	12. jugular
13. credit	13. benevolent	13. biology	13. deflected	13. junction
14. credentials	14. benefactor	14. symbiosis	14. flexible	14. disjointed
15. incredible	15. bonafide	15. biosphere	15. reflected	15. join

Page 59	Page 68	Page 77	Page 86	Page 95
1. a	1. d	1. d	1. a	1. d
2. b	2. a	2. b	2. d	2. b
3. d	3. b	3. a	3. b	3. c
4. a	4. a	4. a	4. a	4. a
5. d	5. c	5. d	5. b	5. a
6. c	6. a	6. a	6. a	6. a
7. a	7. c	7. c	7. a	7. d
8. a	8. a	8. a	8. b	8. b
9. a	9. d	9. a	9. a	9. a
10. a	10. a	10. d	10. a	10. c
11. jury	11. dismal	11. survivor	11. fragile	11. ruptured
12. jurist	12. malady	12. vivid	12. fragment	12. interrupt
13. justice	13. malfeasance	13. vivacious	13. fractured	13. corrupt
14. jurisdiction	14. malnourished	14. vitamins	14. infraction	14. eruptions
15. justify	15. malefactor	15. revitalize	15. fraction	15. disruption

Page 60	Page 69	Page 78	Page 87	Page 96
1. d	1. b	1. d	1. a	1. d
2. a	2. a	2. b	2. c	2. b
3. b	3. d	3. a	3. d	3. a
4. a	4. c	4. b	4. d	4. b
5. b	5. b	5. a	5. b	5. d
6. a	6. c	6. c	6. b	6. c
7. a	7. a	7. c	7. d	7. a
8. a	8. b	8. a	8. a	8. a
9. d	9. d	9. a	9. a	9. a
10. b	10. a	10. a	10. b	10. a
11. a	11. b	11. a	11. a	11. d
12. a	12. a	12. b	12. a	12. a
13. a	13. a	13. a	13. a	13. a
14. d	14. b	14. a	14. d	14. a
15. d	15. a	15. b	15. a	15. d

Answer Key

Page 100
1. b
2. d
3. d
4. b
5. c
6. a
7. a
8. c
9. c
10. a
11. precede
12. proceeded
13. concede
14. exceed
15. recess

Page 104
1. d
2. a
3. a
4. d
5. c
6. a
7. a
8. d
9. b
10. a
11. extroverts
12. introvert
13. anniversary
14. conversation
15. diversion

Page 105
1. d
2. a
3. b
4. b
5. c
6. d
7. b
8. a
9. a
10. a
11. c
12. b
13. d
14. b
15. b

Page 109
1. d
2. d
3. a
4. a
5. d
6. c
7. a
8. b
9. a
10. c
11. contract
12. distract
13. retraction
14. attract
15. abstract

Page 113
1. b
2. a
3. c
4. a
5. d
6. a
7. a
8. a
9. b
10. b
11. construction
12. reconstruct
13. misconstrued
14. obstruction
15. destruction

Page 114
1. a
2. b
3. d
4. a
5. d
6. a
7. b
8. a
9. a
10. c
11. d
12. b
13. a
14. a
15. d

Page 118
1. a
2. d
3. d
4. c
5. a
6. b
7. a
8. a
9. a
10. b
11. therms
12. exothermic
13. thermostat
14. thermos
15. thermophiles

Page 122
1. d
2. a
3. b
4. a
5. a
6. b
7. d
8. a
9. c
10. b
11. social
12. Association
13. disassociate
14. socialites
15. sociology

Page 123
1. b
2. a
3. c
4. d
5. b
6. a
7. a
8. c
9. c
10. a
11. d
12. b
13. a
14. d
15. b

Page 127
1. a
2. b
3. a
4. d
5. d
6. d
7. b
8. c
9. d
10. a
11. cacophony
12. phonics
13. euphonic
14. microphone
15. gramophone

Page 131
1. d
2. b
3. d
4. d
5. b
6. d
7. a
8. a
9. c
10. b
11. restricted
12. string
13. district
14. strain
15. astringent

Page 132
1. d
2. c
3. b
4. a
5. b
6. a
7. d
8. a
9. d
10. a
11. d
12. c
13. a
14. d
15. b

Page 136
1. a
2. d
3. b
4. a
5. d
6. b
7. a
8. c
9. b
10. d
11. geodes
12. terra cotta
13. geologist
14. geography
15. extraterrestrial

Page 140
1. d
2. a
3. a
4. d
5. c
6. d
7. d
8. a
9. c
10. a
11. navigator
12. astronauts
13. nautical
14. nauseous
15. cosmonaut, astronaut

Page 141
1. d
2. a
3. a
4. d
5. d
6. c
7. b
8. a
9. d
10. b
11. a
12. a
13. a
14. d
15. b